Learning Targets

Spelling

Key Stage 2
Scotland P4-P7

John Jackman

Text © John Jackman, 1999
Original illustrations © Nelson Thornes Ltd 1999

The right of John Jackman to be identified as author of this work has been asserted
by him in accordance with the Copyright, Designs and Patents Act 1988.

All rights reserved. The copyright holders authorise ONLY users of *Learning Targets:
Spelling Key Stage 2* to make photocopies of the *copymasters and pages 14-23* for
their own or their students' immediate use within the teaching context. No other
rights are granted without permission in writing from the publishers or under licence
from the Copyright Licensing Agency Limited. Further details of such licences (for
reprographic reproduction) may be obtained from the Copyright Licensing Agency
Limited, of 90 Tottenham Court Road, London W1T 4LP.

Copy by any other means or for any other purpose is strictly prohibited without prior
written consent from the copyright holders. Application for such permission should
be addressed to the publishers.

Any person who commits any unauthorised act in relation to this publication may be
liable to criminal prosecution and civil claims for damages.

First published in 1999 by:
Stanley Thornes (Publishers) Ltd

Reprinted in 2001 by:
Nelson Thornes Ltd
Delta Place
27 Bath Road
CHELTENHAM
GL53 7TH
United Kingdom

05 / 10 9 8

A catalogue record of this book is available from the British Library

ISBN 0 7487 3598 4

Illustrations by Maureen Carter and Sally Michel
Page make-up by GreenGate Publishing Services

Printed and bound in Great Britain by Ashford Colour Press Ltd. Gosport, Hants.

Acknowledgments

The author and publishers wish to thank Dr Joyce Morris for her permission to
publish The Morris-Montessori Word List on page 5.

Extracts from The National Literacy Strategy produced by the Department for
Education and Employment is Crown copyright reproduced with the permission of
the Controller of Her Majesty's Stationery Office.

**Nelson Thornes publishes a comprehensive range of teacher resource books in the *Blueprints* and *Learning
Targets* series. These titles provide busy teachers with unbeatable curriculum coverage, inspiration and value
for money. For a complete list, please call our Primary Customer Services on 01242 267280, send an e-mail to
cservice@nelsonthornes.com or write to:
Nelson Thornes Ltd, Freepost, Primary Customer Services, Delta Place, 27 Bath Road, Cheltenham GL53 7ZZ.
All Nelson Thornes titles can be bought by phone using a credit or debit card on 01242 267280 or online by
visiting our website – www.nelsonthornes.com**

CONTENTS

Welcome to
LEARNING TARGETS

Learning Targets is a series of practical teacher's resource books written to help you to plan and deliver well-structured, professional lessons in line with all the relevant curriculum documents.

Each Learning Target book provides exceptionally clear lesson plans that cover the whole of its stated curriculum plus a large bank of carefully structured copymasters. Links to the key curriculum documents are provided throughout to enable you to plan effectively.

The Learning Targets series has been written in response to the challenge confronting teachers not just to come up with teaching ideas which cover the curriculum but to ensure that they deliver high quality lessons every lesson with the emphasis on raising standards of pupil achievement.

The recent thinking from the QCA and the National Literacy and Numeracy Strategies on the key factors in effective teaching has been built into the structure of Learning Targets. These might briefly be summarised as follows:

➡ that effective teaching is active teaching directed to very clear objectives
➡ that good lessons are delivered with pace, rigour and purpose
➡ that good teaching requires a range of strategies – including interactive whole class sessions
➡ that ongoing formative assessment is essential to planning children's learning
➡ that differentiation is necessary but that it must be realistic.

The emphasis in Learning Targets is on absolute clarity. We have written and designed the books to enable you to access and deliver effective lessons as easily as possible, with the following aims:

➡ to plan and deliver rigorous, well-structured lessons
➡ to set explicit targets for achievement in every lesson that you teach
➡ to make the children aware of what they are going to learn
➡ to put the emphasis on direct, active teaching every time
➡ to make effective use of time and resources
➡ to employ the full range of recommended strategies: whole class, group and individual work
➡ to differentiate for ability groups realistically
➡ to use ongoing formative assessment to plan your next step
➡ to have ready access to usable pupil copymasters to support your teaching.

The following page provides an at-a-glance guide to the key features of the Learning Targets lessons and explains how they will enable you to deliver effective lessons.

How to deliver structured lessons with pace, rigour and purpose

Explicit targets for achievement in every section

The concise subject knowledge you need

Crystal clear lesson plan layouts

The full range of teaching strategies

Rigorous and practical activities

Section 6 — Compound words, contractions and syllabification

Learning targets
On completion of this section children will:
1 ➤ understand the concept of compound words
2 ➤ have practised all the main contractions
3 ➤ have become aware of the concept of syllables.

Before you start
Words can be manipulated, built up and deconstructed in various ways. Various curriculum documents suggest children spend time looking for words within words. However, this should not be confused with compound words, contracted words or word syllables. 'Words within words', is not a linguistic concept, although it is a useful device for encouraging children to think carefully about letter combinations. Thus, 'star' can be said to encompass 'star', 'tar', 'tart' and 'art'.

Background knowledge
Compound words, in their simplest form, are nouns composed of two other nouns which together make a different word (e.g. 'lighthouse' is a combination of the two nouns 'light' and 'house'. Other kinds of words can also be combined to form compound nouns.

Contractions are also usually two (though sometimes one or three) words which are abbreviated in the spoken form. In writing this is represented by an apostrophe. The apostrophe marks the part of the word where letters have been omitted (e.g. 'I am' contracts to 'I'm'). On occasions there are variations on this (e.g. 'cannot' – one word – contracts to 'can't'; 'will not' contracts to 'won't' – notice the letter change).

Syllables are the 'units of pronunciation uttered without interruption forming the whole or part of a word'. Each syllable in a word contains a vowel phoneme and usually one or more consonant sounds (e.g. 'magic' has two syllables 'mag + ic').

Teaching the units

Units 1–8   Copymasters 58–65

This section comprises 8 units:
Unit 1: **Compound words 1** (Copymaster 58)
Unit 2: **Compound words 2** (Copymaster 59)
Unit 3: **Compound words 3** (Copymaster 60)
Unit 4: **Contractions 1** (Copymaster 61)
Unit 5: **Contractions 2** (Copymaster 62)
Unit 6: **Contractions 3** (Copymaster 63)
Unit 7: **Syllables 1** (Copymaster 64)
Unit 8: **Syllables 2** (Copymaster 65)

General teaching strategies
1 To introduce compound words, write the following clues on the board, omitting the words in bold:
finger + print = **fingerprint**
light + house = lighthouse
pass + **word** = password
rail + way = **railway**
Ask the children to supply the missing single or compound words.

112

Invite volunteers to offer similar clues for other compound words.
2 Contractions might be introduced in a rather similar way. Write these examples on the board, omitting the letters in bold:

they are   they're
it is   it's
you will   you'll

Explain that the words in the second column are contractions. They are formed by combining the two words in the first column. Ask a child to describe what has been done to make the contraction. Emphasise that the apostrophe does not float about aimlessly, but is positioned exactly where the missing letter(s) would have been.
3 Point out that contractions are usually associated with informal language situations. They are not usually part of formal or official language. Write the following piece on the board, and ask for a volunteer to read it aloud, substituting contractions for the underlined words. Ask other children to rub out and replace the underlined words with contractions.

We are having a class Christmas party next Monday. We will invite the head teacher as she was not able to come last year. It will be fun. I am sure there will be lots to eat. Let us all think of games we would like to play.

4 Syllables can be understood only if the class has a firm grasp of vowel phonemes. Say your own name, or the name of a child, very slowly and clearly. Ask how many vowel sounds were heard. Follow by asking selected children to say their names slowly and deliberately to the class. Write each name on the board, and use them to distinguish between vowel letters and vowel sounds, e.g. Jane = one vowel sound, but two vowel letters. From this the concept of one vowel sound = one syllable can be developed.
5 Each child should have three pieces of paper, marked 1, 2, 3. Read the following words. After each word the

children should hold up the paper corresponding to the number of vowel sounds/syllables:

breeze bonnet children discover scratch teapot untidy unhelpful chair

6 Discuss the difference between syllables and finding words within words. Use the following words, and others the children might suggest, to undertake both tasks alongside each other to demonstrate the difference.

understand recording reinforcement basket architect chemistry

Group or individual strategies
1 Use the copymasters as appropriate.
2 Give the group a 'starter' word or words from which they have to create as many compound words as possible, e.g.

house: lighthouse greenhouse houseboat treehouse

3 A group or pair of children could make and play 'Contraction Concentration', a simple card game. On one card write a contraction and on another the words from which it was made (e.g. 'haven't', 'have not'). Make about 20 such pairs of cards.
a) Place the cards face down.
b) Each player in turn selects two cards, trying to make a matching pair.
If a pair is found the player keeps them and takes another turn.
c) Play until all the cards are matched and removed.
d) The winner is the player with the most pairs.
4 Write a list of words for the group, e.g.

hat own time thirty peppermint newspaper babies raining happiness happily knitting.

Divide a piece of paper into four columns. Write the words in the first column, the vowel letters they see in the second, the vowels they hear in the third, and the number of syllables in the fourth.

Units 1–3   Compound words

Reference chart of simple compound words and more advanced concepts of compounding words

I   Two words joined together

bedroom	fingerprint	homework	matchbox	spotlight
crossword	fireman	lampshade	playground	tablecloth
dartboard	flashlight	lighthouse	shoelace	
earthquake	foghorn	lipstick	showjumping	
farmhouse	football	manhole	skateboard	

113

Linked copymasters for differentiated practice and assessment

Useful lists of spelling groups included

---

64   name ___   date ___

A syllable is a part of a word that can be sounded by itself.
Every syllable has a vowel sound.

Say these words to yourself.
Write how many syllables you hear.

turkey (tur-key) [2]   monkey ☐
garden ☐   fork ☐
finger ☐   kangaroo ☐
computer ☐   nose ☐
circus ☐   railway ☐

Write the syllables for each of these words.

happy   hap-py   silly ___
birthday ___   Thursday ___
fourteen ___   yesterday ___
tomorrow ___   Saturday ___
unhappy ___   impossible ___

Choose four long words from a book, and write out the syllables in each.
___
___

SYLLABLES 1   122   Learning Targets: Spelling Key Stage 2

---

65   name ___   date ___

...e is a part of a word that can be sounded by itself.
...ble has a vowel sound.

... words to yourself. Write how many syllables you hear.

...-ple) [2]   person ☐
                undone ☐
                difficult ☐
                crocodile ☐
                purple ☐

...ble in the first column to a syllable in the second
...ake a word.

...ng	broth	cle
...y	gar	er
	un	son
April	per	den

	in	en
...e	farm	cket
	gw	side
	cri	er

123   Learning Targets: Spelling Key Stage 2

INTRODUCTION

Learning Targets: *Spelling Key Stage* 2 offers a complete structured resource for the teaching of spelling and related word level skills at Key Stage 2, ages 7–11 (P4–P7 in Scotland). Its coverage is consistent with the requirements of the National Literacy Strategy, though it goes far beyond the specific requirements. It puts the NLS into a framework which enables teachers to develop a thorough and structured programme for their pupils.

The book discusses the range of approaches to the teaching of spelling. This is followed by eight sections:

1   General activities
2   Key regular long vowel spellings
3   Irregular, or variable, grapheme/phoneme relationships, including homophones
4   Other significant clusters/strings
5   Silent letters
6   Compound words, contractions and syllabification
7   Roots and suffixes, including plurals
8   Roots and prefixes, including antonyms

Section 1 General activities provides a range of copymasters which have been designed to support particular approaches recommended in the NLS *Framework for Teaching*. These include a photocopiable personal spelling log which contains all the NLS high and medium frequency words and allows the children to collect their own words to use in their writing. Also provided on pages 18–23 are photocopiable word lists for children to use, often as part of a homework assignment, devised to promote the LSCWC strategy. These words have been carefully arranged to enable the pupils to benefit as much as possible from another suggested approach, namely learning how to spell words by analogy. There is also support for dictionary-based work.

Sections 2 to 8 provide a progressive range of suggestions and work within each category of spelling requirement. Thus, whilst the NLS document refers simply to 'spelling of the words containing each of the long vowel phonemes', this book will offer particular suggestions for the coverage this implies and how it might be thoroughly yet flexibly delivered to classes with a wide range of spelling ability.

The arrangement of the material in this *Learning Targets* book is necessarily different from most of the other titles in the series. However, it will provide a valuable resource, whether you choose to develop parts of the material as complete literacy hour lessons, or simply to incorporate the work into other literacy hour themes.

This book will enable you to:

- plan and deliver structured lessons on spelling as part of your overall literacy programme
- teach all the sight vocabulary required by the National Literacy Strategy (but basic for all children in the age group)
- assess the children's progress along the way.

Using the sections

Each section begins by setting out the learning targets and any essential background knowledge you need to have at your fingertips. Each section comprises a sequence of units which deliver the learning targets. Due to the nature of spelling teaching, the suggested methods for teaching the various skills follow a similar pattern. Therefore you will find that the beginning of each section sets out the teaching suggestions in detail and you will need to refer back to these as you work through the units.

A whole lesson will not normally be devoted to word level learning. Usually, from other resources available, the teacher will use the first 10–15 minutes as a whole class reading and writing session, based upon a shared text or a collaborative writing task. *Learning Targets*: *Reading and Writing* and *Learning Targets*: *Grammar and Punctuation* provide structured activities for text level and sentence level work respectively. You will find that work at these other levels can lead naturally into a relevant unit of work in this book; for example choosing a reading activity which is rich in a particular phoneme or grapheme will allow you to select word level work from this book.

Word lists

In addition to the teaching suggestions you will also find resource lists of words as and where appropriate.

These provide you with an extra and invaluable resource for word level teaching.

Useful family word groups

Teachers have reported that they find it invaluable to have at-a-glance lists of the kinds of words which relate to a particular spelling pattern or rule. It can be extremely time consuming to assemble lists of words to demonstrate what you are teaching. These lists do the work for you. Whilst most of us can think of a number of words for a particular spelling group or rule immediately, it can be disruptive to the teaching flow if carefully considered vocabulary is not readily to hand. And whilst it may be possible to call to mind words with an appropriate pattern, it is not easy to grade such words and to eliminate those which also include components that are either irregular or have not been taught yet. At the heart of systematic teaching is the need for rigour in eliminating as many as possible of the hurdles that can trip up the children.

'Little and often' is a good maxim for teaching spelling. Avoid giving children long lists to learn. You can use the word lists to give children short lists of words to learn to spell. Try to ensure that each child succeeds most of the time, and avoid introducing 'irregular' variants of a pattern before the 'regular' form has been thoroughly internalised.

Related National Literacy Strategy sight words

Opportunities are provided to introduce all the sight vocabulary that primary-aged children should know, as defined by the National Literacy Strategy, in a systematic and logical way. Many units include lists of these words and the words also appear as photocopiable 'LSCWC' lists. The aim of including these words is to suggest relevant opportunities to introduce the sight vocabulary at appropriate moments. Although the actual lists are drawn from the National Literacy Strategy they are essential words for all children in the age range to know. These lists of sight vocabulary provide a systematic and logical way of accumulating sight vocabulary whilst learning the spelling rules and patterns.

Using the copymasters

To support the teaching ideas, each section concludes with a bank of copymasters. The copymasters are not intended solely for direct photocopiable use: they also demonstrate how activities can be developed with the whole class, or with groups or individuals. In many cases an activity from one copymaster might be adapted to teach a quite different skill. The copymasters have two other important functions:

1 *Assessment* It can sometimes be difficult to evaluate confidently the progress of each individual child. Vigilance is required to spot any child in a group situation being carried along by his or her peers without having mastered a particular skill. If carefully administered, the copymasters can help to alleviate this problem and alert you to where a little extra intervention is required.

2 *Homework* Depending on the school policy, the copymasters can readily be used for homework tasks. This will allow parents to gain an insight into the underlying systematic approach to spelling which is being used. As well as the copymasters the children may be given small 'sets' of related words to learn at home. These can be derived from the word lists for each unit. Spelling needs constant practice – 'little and often' should be the approach. Thus a regular spot in the homework schedule is valuable. However, children will soon become aware that this is a 'soft option' unless regular testing of the homework tasks occurs.

A brief review of methods and approaches

Is spelling 'caught' or 'taught'? That it to say, is mere exposure to words in print sufficient for a child to learn to spell, or is faster and more sustainable progress achieved by a structured approach to the teaching of the discrete skills associated with spelling? This question is of fundamental importance to primary years teachers.

There is no question where the NLS stands, and it is a position endorsed by the experience of this author. Research has shown that whilst some children may achieve some improvement in their ability to spell as a spin-off from their reading, this is by no means true for less 'focused' readers. Even 'careful' readers are unlikely to gain full mastery of spelling without other, more struc- tured, inputs to the teaching and correction of spelling errors.

Two further questions then arise. Is there one 'best' way to teach spelling? What are the main aspects of language that a teacher embarking on creating a balanced spelling programme should take into account and seek to encourage?

The following is a résumé of the main methodologies adopted for the teaching of spelling.

1 The use and development of memory

Visual memory

Most adults are able to hold large numbers of visual pat- terns in their memory. Despite the huge number of possible variations, most of us are able to recognise when a particular string of letters doesn't 'look right'. Such 'serial probability' is an important component in our learning to spell, and this is developed more quickly if children are systematically and thoroughly exposed to the common phonemically regular patterns, to which they can add, in an organised way, the less frequent or irregular occurrences.

Auditory memory

It has been shown that for some children, visual memory alone is not enough. The ability to discriminate through hearing is as important as visual discrimination when it comes to mastery of spelling. The process of working on sound/symbol relationships of a phonic programme to underpin early reading can have the spin-off benefit of helping with the visual and aural memory required for early spelling proficiency.

Memory-related teaching strategies

Look-say-cover-write-check

A well-tried and effective technique to help with the memorising of individual and groups of words is *look – say – cover – write – check*. This is a proven technique which is recommended in a number of national curriculum doc- uments. It can be used at various levels, and for regular as well as irregular word spellings. There is a series of copymasters (pages 18–23) that are designed to support this approach with particular regard to the NLS sight recognition words.

Visual and aural memory can often be slow to develop in young children and less gifted older children. For these, support with the grouping of words with similar letter strings and sounds can be especially important. The key is to avoid discouraging the children by demanding too much. Imagine being asked to remember a dozen or more words from a foreign language. Clearly, it would be considerably easier if you were given the words in small, visually similar, groups. The same is true for children learning to spell. Most will achieve greater success if they memorise little and often.

Spelling and handwriting

Professor Fred Schonell stressed that the 'visual, audi- tory and articulatory elements must be firmly cemented in writing'. This has been supported by subsequent research, and, empirically, by many teachers. Not only can the use of handwriting help to reinforce the spelling of groups of words with similar letter strings, but the handwriting practice offered is in itself a valuable and useful activity. 'Handwriting' does not have to imply a well-developed facility to write in a joined style, although the sooner this skill is mastered the better from the point of view of helping the child hold patterns of letter strings in mind.

Mnemonics

Whilst the use of *look – say – cover – write – check* and hand- writing are the main approaches to aid the development of memory, there are others. Although mnemonic trickery cannot seriously of itself underpin a spelling programme, in its place it can have useful, if limited, applications, especially with those one-off problem words! (Remembering the *cess* pit in the middle, means you'll never again misspell 'necessary'!)

2 The development of understanding

Appreciating the sound/symbol relationships

English has 44 sounds (phonemes) variously represented by 26 letters (graphemes).

Spoken	Written
24 consonant sounds	**21** consonant letters
20 vowel sounds	**5** vowel letters
44 speech sounds	**26** alphabet letters

Dr Joyce Morris has exemplified the 44 phonemes with reference to the words in the table on page 5, presup- posing a standard English dialect (as used in the *Everyman English Pronouncing Dictionary*).

For the majority of words in English we spell as we sound and hear, so, if thoroughly learnt, the patterns and combinations exemplified in the table above give a good, sound foundation on which to build. However, it should be remembered that in many regions children will not be accustomed to hearing or using some standard pronunciation.

Consonant sounds		Vowel sounds	
1	**b**ed	1	**c**at
2	**c**at; **k**id; so**ck**	2	h**e**n
3	**d**og	3	k**i**d
4	**f**an	4	d**o**g
5	**g**um	5	s**u**n
6	**h**en	6	c**a**pe; s**ai**l; h**ay**
7	**j**et	7	b**ee**; l**ea**f
8	**l**og	8	k**i**te; t**ie**; fl**y**; l**igh**t
9	**m**op	9	r**o**se; b**oa**t; t**oe**
10	**n**et	10	m**oo**n; l**u**te; bl**ue**; scr**ew**
11	**p**up	11	b**oo**k
12	**r**od	12	s**aw**; v**au**lt; b**all**; f**or**k; c**ore**
13	**s**un	13	c**ar**
14	**t**ub	14	g**ir**l; c**ur**l; f**er**n
15	**v**an	15	h**ou**se; c**ow**
16	**w**ig	16	c**oi**n; b**oy**
17	**y**ak	17	h**are**; f**air**
18	**z**ip	18	**ear**; d**eer**; h**ere**
19	ri**ng**; si**nk**	19	p**oor**; l**ure**
20	**sh**op	20	lett**er**
21	**ch**imp		
22	**th**en		
23	**th**umb		
24	televi**si**on		

The Morris–Montessori Word List © Dr. Joyce Morris from *English Words listed according to 'Phonics 44' the research-based linguistics informed system for initial literacy* published by the London Montessori Centre Ltd., 18 Balderton St, London, W1Y 1TG.

There is a growing body of evidence that children progress faster in reading and other language skills if a structured phonics programme is followed. Children begin to accumulate language skills – first oral and aural – from a very early age. Once exposed to print, other snippets of visual language knowledge begin to be assembled by the child, albeit randomly. But the sooner the teacher can begin to give pattern and meaning to the language learning processes, the more rapid and effective will be the assimilation of knowledge.

Analogy
Although reading is a decoding process and spelling an encoding process, and although, as previously acknowledged, there are significant mismatches in the sound/symbol correspondences, there is enough common ground for the teaching strategies of the two language skills to be beneficially planned in parallel. Indeed, many teachers have testified to the advantages that accrue to spelling from a well-planned phonics programme primarily designed for helping with early reading skills. Support

for this view has in recent years been given also by Goswami and Bryant. They have described that whilst reading and spelling seem to develop independently in the first two years, through the Key Stage 2 years a change occurs and the two processes definitely seem to facilitate one another. As they note:

> It is probably a short intellectual step from knowing that 'light', 'fight', 'sight' and 'tight' all end in the same sound, to understanding that that is why they all share a common spelling pattern.

But the importance and value of well-planned and carefully structured teaching of phonics does not benefit only the younger child. Where there are special needs for additional support with reading for older children, a structured and organised phonemic emphasis on spelling can, and often does, have the extra advantage of supporting a remedial reading programme.

Word morphology
Morphology is about word structure and is concerned with the parts of the word that carry meaning, particularly roots and their suffixes and prefixes. It is important, when learning to apply the relatively few rules of English spelling, to understand the morphology of the words to which the rules are applied. To understand how to spell 'happily', it helps to know that it comprises the frequently used suffix 'ly' and the root happy, in which the 'y' has followed the rule (see page 8) and been changed to an 'i'.

How an awareness and understanding of the principles of morphology can help with good spelling can also be seen in the context of compound words and contractions. A significant number of the words most frequently written by 7-year olds are compound, such as 'sometimes', 'something', 'outside', 'football' and 'birthday'. Also, contractions such as 'don't' and 'didn't' are frequently used by young writers, so once they understand how such words are constructed, problems of remembering when and where to put the apostrophe and which letters are omitted begin to vanish.

Etymology
A long history of language influxes has led English to develop into the form we speak and write today. Latin (together with its own Greek influences) had been introduced with the Romans and subsequently many other language 'importations' have come to contribute to our modern English words and spelling. Not only is this interesting for children to realise, but a recognition of the place of specific letter strings in our spelling, such as 'phy' from Greek, can be helpful.

Syllabification
Morphology and syllabification are different. Whilst morphology relates to meaning, syllabification relates to the speech *impulses* of a word. The two should not be confused. Morphologically the word 'development' comprises the root 'develop' and the suffix 'ment'. However, when split into speech impulses, or syllables, it might be split 'de - vel - op - ment'. Understanding and appreciating both aspects of word composition is important. Each plays an important part in spelling, but it helps to be aware of the important distinction between them. Syllables often comprise useful 'chunks' of words

that are more easily recalled than strings of individual letters.

Semantics and syntax

An awareness of semantics (word meaning) and syntax (grammatical structure) becomes significant in such contexts as deciding between the homophones 'their' and 'there', and later in whether or when to spell 'practice' with a 'c' or an 's'.

A co-operative approach to spelling

A planned policy

A school policy should be evolved which defines the approach to the teaching of spelling, the methodologies to be used, and the organisation and management of supporting resources within the school environment, and which establishes in the minds of the children when accurate spelling matters and when it is less important.

No systematised scheme, however carefully planned and implemented, can possibly eliminate the requirement for sensitive correction of errors in presented work, with the opportunities that this offers for diagnosis and subsequent teaching. Nor can it anticipate the opportunities for spelling lessons for individuals, groups or the whole class based on another literacy theme or topic, or indeed an opportunity that lends itself fortuitously during the teaching of another subject.

Class, group, individual teaching

A good teacher will develop parallel strategies for both class/group teaching and individual teaching of spelling. Whether or not class teaching is eventually shown to have a distinct advantage over other strategies, one thing is sure – in terms of overall teacher efficiency there must be a place for whole class teaching of spelling. It is equally important to recognise that this need not imply that all the children should be working on the same material. It is possible for the teacher to lead structured lessons but with children working more or less at their own pace. In reality there are usually advantages to keeping groups of children working at the same pace, so that additional related activities that suggest themselves can be worked on by several pupils together.

Encouraging independence in spelling

It is simply impossible in a busy and purposeful classroom for the teacher to be readily available to offer 'spellings' as required to every child at the moment of need. The children need to see the teacher as a support, but not a first resort. Whilst the importance of accurate spelling should always be stressed and encouraged, a careful balance must be struck to avoid possible 'spelling failure' which would inhibit children's written work. In pre-presentation drafting reasonable attempts at spelling should always be positively acknowledged and respected, never criticised. But whilst the fresh flow of well-expressed ideas is of crucial importance for quality writing, when 'going public' the importance of quality of presentation – including spelling – needs to be recognised by all the children. The object is to engender pride in well-presented work in whatever field.

It is important for the teacher to be constantly alert to patterns of spelling difficulty. If a type of error constantly recurs it could be useful to give the child a list of similar words with the same letter pattern to learn and practise. Such learning by analogy is an approach this programme has been devised to offer, amongst others.

We should constantly be seeking to help the children to achieve independence in spelling. It is strongly recommended that 'spelling support' should be a permanent feature of every classroom or work area. This might include the provision of lists, probably on the wall or in readily available folders, of 'difficult' words which have a high frequency and are likely to be of use in the context of current class topics from across the curriculum, but which because of their complexity will not normally have been internalised at a particular age. The wall display might also feature one or more of the letter patterns which have been the focus of recent lessons. Dictionaries and word books appropriate to the age range should also always be available, as should one or more thesauruses, but no type of reference book is of help unless the children become confident in using it! (This programme offers some opportunities for basic dictionary skills practice, but there is no substitute for constant practice, whenever there are few minutes to spare.)

When using word processors, it should be considered a mortal sin for a child presenting work on a word processor which has a spell-checker facility, for the spellings not to have been checked! However, they should bear in mind that a spell checker cannot distinguish between homophones. Computers can also be used as extensions to the spelling reference resources mentioned above. Some software provides word lists that can be scrolled through alphabetically, and some dictionaries are available on CD-ROM. At the very least a word processor with a spell-checking facility will enable the child to type in the required word to see whether his or her spelling is correct, or to be offered alternatives.

Home-school links

Spelling is one of the areas where home support can enhance the effectiveness and speed of learning but, as with reading, great care is needed in briefing parents. The aim is to achieve the one-to-one support that a sensible adult can provide, but too much pressure of the wrong sort can become counter-productive. Teachers using this programme will make their own decisions, but most, if not all, will lend itself to use for homework assignments.

There are other ways in which parent support can be encouraged, including:

- calling attention to other words that have a similar letter string to those recently practised – especially in environmental print contexts

- always being available to *write down* words needed in the course of written work at home – then testing them using the LSCWC method

- praising good effort in spelling, especially if any error is a phonemically 'reasonable' attempt, before correcting

- playing spelling games, such as finding small words within longer words and collecting as many words as possible with a given letter string.

In conclusion, what is most important is that a school spelling policy is agreed and signed-up to by all the staff. This might cover:

- the agreed spelling philosophy and strategy
- the use of structured materials
- other spelling support materials required for each classroom and work area
- the role of parents
- coping with children with particular spelling needs.

The main rules of English spelling

As already mentioned, most spelling rules are related to an understanding of morphology (roots, suffixes and prefixes, contractions, compound words, plural constructions) and etymology (origins, meanings, foreign words).

The following list, whilst not exclusive, represents the main useful rules. It is suggested that these might be introduced in particular circumstances with individual children, though on occasions it may be appropriate to build a class or group lesson around a particular rule. As they are best introduced as part of a structured course, it is suggested that they be referred to as and when relevant rather than being taught intensively over a short period.

The rules marked with an asterisk are those specifically recommended in the Scottish Guidelines *English Language 5–14*.

It is of paramount importance always to bear in mind that nearly every spelling rule has its exceptions. Nevertheless, a knowledge of rules can significantly improve the chances of spelling a word correctly.

General rules

1 'q' is never written without 'u'   (queen)
2* No English words end with 'j' or 'v' (except 'spiv'), and very few end with 'i'.
3 'ee' or long 'i' sounds at the end of a word are usually represented by 'y'   (happy;   my)
4* The 'k' sound after a short vowel is usually written 'ck'   (pack;   wreck)
   (except multisyllable words ending in 'ic': terrific).
5* 'i' comes before 'e' (when the sound is 'ee')   (piece; priest)
   except after 'c'   (receive; ceiling; receipt)
   or when the sound is not 'ee'   (eight; reign; heir)
6 If a noun ends in '-ce' and the verb is formed from the same root, the verb usually ends in '-se' (practice/practise; advice/advise; licence/license)

Using suffixes

1* To add a suffix when a word ends with 'e':
   drop the 'e' if the suffix begins with a vowel or is 'y'
   (ice/icing/icy)
   keep the 'e' if the suffix begins with a consonant
   (wake/wakeful)
   (Some exceptions: true/truly; argue/argument;
   due/duly)

2 To add the suffix 'able' or 'ous' to a word that ends in
   '-ce' or '-ge'
   retain the 'e' to keep the 'c' or 'g' soft
   (notice/noticeable; manage/manageable;
   outrage/outrageous)

3* To add a suffix to a short word, or a word where the
   last syllable is stressed, look at the letter before the
   last:
   ● if it is a single vowel, we normally double the last
     letter before adding the suffix
     (hop/hopping/hopped; transmit/transmitter)
   ● if it is not a single vowel, or the last syllable is not
     stressed, we normally just add the suffix
     (sing/singing; read/reading; profit/profited)
   Note: 'w', 'x' and 'y' are never doubled.

4 To add a suffix when a word ends with 'y' (that
   sounds 'ee'):
   change the 'y' to an 'i' before adding the suffix
   (ugly/ugliness)

5* 'ul' or 'il' at the end of a word only have one 'l'
   (spoonful; until)

6 'able' is a five-times more frequent suffix than 'ible',
   especially if the antonym (opposite) begins with 'un'
   (reliable/unreliable; resistible/irresistible)

Using prefixes

1 To add a prefix just do it! (Don't adjust for double
   letters.)
   (un+sure/unsure; mis+spelt/misspelt;
   im+moral/immoral)

2 'al' at the beginning of a word only has one 'l'   (also;
   always)
   – and remember, all right is two words!

Making plurals

1 To make the plural form of most nouns, we just add
   's' (goat/goats; shop/shops)

2 To make the plural form of nouns ending in 's', 'x',
   'sh' or 'ch' we add 'es'   (bus/buses; bush/bushes).

3 To make the plural form of nouns that end in a
   consonant + 'y'
   we change 'y' to 'i' and add 'es'   (baby/babies)

4 To make the plural form of nouns that end in a vowel
   + 'y' we just add 's'   (day/days).

5 To make the plural form of nouns that end in 'f' or
   'fe', we normally change the 'f' or 'fe' to 'v' and add
   'es'   (wolf/wolves; wife/wives)

6 To make the plural form of nouns that end in 'o', we
   normally add 'es'   (hero/heroes; volcano/volcanoes)
   unless they end in 'oo', or are music words, or are
   shortened forms (cuckoo/cuckoos; cello/cellos;
   photo/photos)

GLOSSARY

Useful terms relating to spelling

Affixes — Prefixes and suffixes which are added to word roots, e.g. '**dis**cover**ed**'.

Auditory memory — Short-term memory of sound-letter relationships.

Blending — The smooth running together of individual sounds, usually referring to consonant blends, e.g. '**cl**ap', 'sa**nd**', '**str**ap'.

c — Abbreviation for 'consonant' as in '**cvc**' meaning consonent-vowel-consonant.

Consonants — The letters and letter sounds which are not vowels.

Cue — The clues used to help identify a word. These can be 'phonic', 'grammatical' (predictable word ordering) or 'semantic' (predictable from meaning).

Decoding — Translating print into spoken words.

Digraph — A string of letters, usually a pair, which operate together to represent a single sound, e.g. 'br**ow**n' '**sh**op'.
vowel digraph A digraph which represents a single vowel sound, e.g. '**ar**', '**ee**', '**oo**'.
consonant digraph A digraph which represents a single consonant sound, e.g. '**ch**', '**th**', '**sh**'.

Etymology — Word origins and roots.

Grapheme — The written form of the smallest sound segment of a word, e.g. individual letters or digraphs.

Homophones — Words that have the same sound but have different spellings and meanings, e.g. 'there', 'their'.

Homonyms — Words with the same spelling pattern and sometimes the same sound but which have a different meaning, e.g. 'bank' (for financial transactions) and 'bank' (of a river)

Inflections — The endings of verbs which indicate tense, e.g. 'walk**ed**, 'walk**ing**'; or the endings of nouns to indicate plurals, e.g. 'cat**s**', 'fox**es**'.

Mnemonics — Memory joggers.

Morphology — The study of the structures within words which carry elements of the meaning.

Onset — The part of a word or syllable which comes before the vowel sound, e.g. '**cl**' in '**cl**ot'.

Orthographic — To do with spelling.

Position — Within a word, position is often defined as:
'initial' (**sl**eep)
'medial' (sl**ee**p)
'final' (slee**p**)

Phoneme — The spoken form of the smallest sound unit of a word, e.g. individual letter sounds or digraph sounds.

Phonemic — The approach to spelling based on sound-symbol relationships.

Phonics — The relationship between the spoken and written forms of words.

Prefix — An affix added to the beginning of a word to change or modify its meaning, e.g. '**un**fortunate'.

Rhyme — Identity of sound, though not necessarily letter pattern, between words or at the endings of words.

Rime — The part of a word or syllable which comprises the vowel sound and subsequent consonant sound, e.g. '**ot**' in 'cl**ot**'.

Segmentation — The process of identifying constituent parts of words.

Stem — The core part of a verb, to which inflections may be added as required, e.g.'**walk**', '**walk**ed'.

Suffix — An affix added to the end of a word to change or modify its meaning, e.g. 'walk**ed**'.

Syllable — Part of a word including a vowel and its attached consonant sounds.

Tactile — Related to the sense of touch.

v — Abbreviation for vowel as in 'c**v**c' meaning consonant-vowel-consonant.

Vowels — The sounds at the heart of every syllable that are represented by '**a**', '**e**', '**i**', '**o**', '**u**' and sometimes '**y**'.

Whole-word approaches — The rote memorising of individual words.

A curriculum for spelling at KS2

Note: This table offers a suggested curriculum for delivering the main requirements for spelling in the Framework for Literacy. Its organisation and structure reflects the approach of this Learning Targets programme.

	Y3 Term 1	Y3 Term 2	Y3 Term 3	Y4 Term 1	Y4 Term 2
SECTION 2 Key regular long vowel spellings	long vowels: a-e; ai; ay ee; ea	long vowels: i-e; ie; y (fly); igh	long vowels: o-e; oa; oe u-e; ue; oo; ew	long vowels: ar air; are al; aw; au, or	long vowels: ir; ur; er
SECTION 3 Irregular, or variable, grapheme /phoneme relationships including homophones	ea (head); homophones: here; hear to; two; too	y (nappy) homophones: see; sea right; write	oo (foot) 'irregular' magic e homophones: by; buy blue / blew	ask; ast; ass other common homophones	ire; ure; ere -ild -ind -old
SECTION 4 Other significant clusters/strings	-ack -eck -ang -ing -ank -ink -unk l blends r blends s blends inc. str spr spl	sh; ch; th; wh	nch; tch	double consonants; ss ll ff tt	et endings qu
SECTION 5 Silent letters		k g w		final b	w
SECTION 6 Compound words contractions and syllabification	discriminate syllables	simple compound words contractions	short words in long words contractions	more simple compound words	discriminate syllables
SECTION 7 Roots and suffixes, including plurals	+ing rules	making plurals using 'singular'/ 'plural' roots + suffixes +er +est + y -ly -ful -less	making plurals using 'singular' / 'plural' roots + suffixes +er +est -ly -ful -less	to change tense s / ing / ed more suffixes -hood -ness -ment -dom	making plurals words ending in 'f' using 'singular' / 'plural' suffix -sure -ture
SECTION 8 Roots and prefixes, including antonyms	making antonyms -un -re-	making antonyms un- dis-			al-
STRATEGIES & LIST WORDS	NLS Appendix 1 LSCWC spelling log ordering (1st/2nd letter)	NLS Appendix 1 LSCWC dict: alphabetical ordering (mixed 1st/2nd letter)	NLS Appendix 1 LSCWC dict: alphabetical ordering	NLS Appendix 2 LSCWC dict: guide words	NLS Appendix 2 LSCWC dict: alphabetical ordering (up to five letters)

Y4 Term 3	Y5 Term 1	Y5 Term 2	Y5 Term 3	Y6 Term 1	Y6 Term 2 + Term 3
long vowels: *oi; oy* *ow; ou*					
ough *ow (tow)* *o as u*		*further common* *homophones, inc* *eight ate;* *great grate;* *rain rein reign* *weather whether*			*mnemonics*
wa	*-et endings*	*soft c soft g*	*-dge* *ie ei* *-al -el -le* *-en -on*	*-ar -er -or* *-ey*	
general review		*general review*			
advanced *compound* *words* *more contractions* *e.g. it's*			*unstressed vowels* *in polysyllabic* *words*		*unstressed vowels* *in polysyllabic* *words*
collect/classify *common roots +* *origins* *ible / able* *-ive -tion -sion*	*rules for* *pluralisation*	*'ll' becomes* *'l' in suffix*	*suffixing rules* *function of* *suffix: tenses,* *comparatives,* *verbs to nouns,* *nouns to* *verbs etc.*	*origins and* *derivations*	*origins and* *derivations*
un- over- dis- *im-*	*auto- bi- trans-* *tele- circum-*		*negation* *in- im- ir- il-* *pro- sus-*	*aero- aqua- audi- bi-* *con- cred- duo- in-* *micro- oct- photo-* *port- prim- sub- tele-* *tri- ex-*	*origins and* *derivations*
NLS Appendix 2 *LSCWC* *dict definitions*	*NLS Appendix 2* *LSCWC* *using IT spell* *checks inc.* *American spellings*	*NLS Appendix 2* *LSCWC*	*NLS Appendix 2* *(review)*		

Scottish guidelines planner

There are no detailed directions for phonics and spelling against which the content of this book can be closely correlated. It does, however, provide for the central requirements of English Language 5–14 on phonics and spelling as noted below.

WRITING

Level B/Level C

The teaching of spelling should be part of an agreed scheme and a whole-school policy. Supporting use should be made of a published spelling scheme graduated according to pupils' progress. The school should decide on one method of teaching pupils to deal with mistakes. Look-say-cover-write-check is one example from several. The learning of spelling rules should support this. The six most useful spelling rules are set out in SCCC's Responding to Children's Writing, page 60. Pupils should learn to spell words which they need to use frequently in their own writing. A personal spelling book for words causing difficulty becomes both a reference for the pupil and a record for the teacher. After drafting, pupils should mark possible errors, and check and correct spellings using a wordbank or dictionary.

Level D/Level E

Across the curriculum ways of dealing with spelling, and rules for spelling, should now be established. These should include dealing with errors, self-correction techniques, and visual approaches. Individuals should also be expected to compile their own lists, including specialist vocabulary from different curricular areas. The use of a dictionary and a thesaurus, and the routine checking of spelling at the end of drafting, should be actively promoted. Pupils should be helped to see themselves as self-supporting spellers. Teaching about common prefixes, stems and suffixes, related to meanings, will help in this. The use of a graduated spelling scheme should continue where pupils' spelling needs regular reinforcement.

General activities

Learning targets

On completion of this section children will:

1 ➡️ have started a spelling log containing all the 'essential' words suggested in the NLS framework document (see Appendices)
2 ➡️ have practised and begun to acquire proficiency through using the LSCWC methodology, the essential words
3 ➡️ have followed a basic course in dictionary structure and organisation.

Before you start

Section 1 is essentially different in kind from the following sections. It is provided at the beginning to enable you to establish with the children certain approaches to the development of spelling skills.

1 It is recommended that each child should use a personal spelling log. Pages 14–17 will make up into such a booklet, already providing all the high and medium frequency words from the NLS lists. The child should add to this base their own words as needed, and in so doing will be developing important alphabetical skills required in the related activites of referring to dictionaries and other alphabetically arranged texts.

2 The LSCWC lists are photocopiable and, as with the Spelling Log words, derived from the high and medium frequency words from the NLS lists. They have, however, been arranged with regard to spelling 'logic' as far as possible. The children might be given the photocopied lists as homework activities, though it is recommended that preliminary work, using the folding format of the strips, be undertaken in the classroom first. In this way maximum benefit will be derived from the system. There is, of course, no reason why children should not be given any particular group(s) of words to work on more than once. To maximise the effectiveness of this approach, it is clearly important for there to be reasonably careful simple record-keeping in place.

3 Copymasters 1–7 for practising dictionary skills are graded, and largely exemplary. Some children will need considerably more practice than can be offered here, and such additional practice can be easily structured using a similar format. In addition, regular class and group activites related to the use of dictionaries will provide considerable benefits and support those who are finding the tasks less easy to master. Keep the classwork fun – it can provide a useful and enjoyable 'filler'.

To make the booklet photocopy pages 14–17. Fold each page along the dashed horizontal line and place them on top of each other, checking the booklet pages run consecutively before folding in half along the dashed centre line. You can secure the booklet with staples.

world
would
wouldn't
write

....

....

....

....

....

X x

....

....

....

Y y

year
yellow
yes
young
your

....

....

....

....

....

Z z

....

....

Spelling Log

Name ....

Class ....

16

15

A a

about
above
across
after
again
almost
along
also
always
an
animals
another
any
April
around
as

asked
August

B b

baby
back
ball
balloon

....

....

....

....

....

2

V v

very

....

....

....

W w

walk
walked
walking
want
watch
water
way
Wednesday

were
what
when
where
while
white
who
whole
why
will
window
with
without
woke
woken
word
work

can
can't
change
children
clothes
coming
could
couldn't

....
....
....
....
....
....
....

(4)

D d

December
did
didn't
different
do
does
don't
door
down
during

....
....
....

Sunday
sure
swimming

....
....
....
....
....
....
....
....
....

(13)

T t

take
than
that
their
them
then
there
these
think
thirteen
those
thought
three
through
Thursday
time

---

(3)

be
because
bed
been
before
began
being
below
better
between
birthday
black
blue
both
boy
brother
brought
brown
but
by

C c

call
called
came

....
....
....
....
....
....
....

(14)

U u

under
until
upon
us
used

....
....
....
....

....
....
....

today
together
told
ton
too
took
tree
tries
Tuesday
turn
turned
twelve
twenty
two

G g

garden
girl
goes
gone
good
got
great
green
grey

....

....

H h

had
half
happy
has
have
head
heard
her
high

P p

paper
people
pink
place
pull
purple
push
put

....

Q q

....

....

R r

ran
red
right
round

....

F f

father
February
fifteen
first
five
follow
following
found
four
fourteen
Friday
friends
from

E e

....

....

earth
eight
eighteen
eleven
every
eyes

....

....

....

S s

....

....

....

....

Saturday
saw
school
second
seen
September
seven

seventeen
should
show
sister
six
sixteen
small
so
some
something
sometimes
sound
started
still
stopped
such
suddenly

I i

if
I'm

J j

January
July
jump
jumped
June
just

him
his
home
house
how

important
inside

K k

knew
know

L l

lady
last
laugh
leave
liked
little
live
lived
love
loved

M m

made
make
man
many
March
may
May
might
Monday
money
more
morning

mother
much
must

N n

name
near
never
new

next
night
nine
nineteen
not
November
now
number

O o

October
of
off
often
old
once
one
only
opened
or
orange
other
our
out
outside
over
own

LOOK, SAY, COVER	WRITE	CHECK
above	....	....
across	....	....
along	....	....
around	....	....

LOOK, SAY, COVER	WRITE	CHECK
almost	....	....
also	....	....
always	....	....
small	....	....
walk	....	....
animals	....	....

LOOK, SAY, COVER	WRITE	CHECK
still	....	....
follow	....	....
balloon	....	....
happy	....	....
stopped	....	....
suddenly	....	....
swimming	....	....
different	....	....
better	....	....

LOOK, SAY, COVER	WRITE	CHECK
through	....	....
those	....	....
think	....	....
other	....	....
brother	....	....
mother	....	....
father	....	....

LOOK, SAY, COVER	WRITE	CHECK
before	....	....
began	....	....
below	....	....
between	....	....

LOOK, SAY, COVER	WRITE	CHECK
other	....	....
brother	....	....
sister	....	....
mother	....	....
father	....	....

LOOK, SAY, COVER	WRITE	CHECK
never	....	....
number	....	....
paper	....	....
together	....	....
better	....	....
under	....	....

LOOK, SAY, COVER	WRITE	CHECK
together	....	....
clothes	....	....
birthday	....	....
both	....	....
earth	....	....
something	....	....

LOOK, SAY, COVER	WRITE	CHECK
thought	....	....
brought	....	....
through	....	....
before	....	....
important	....	....

© Stanley Thornes (Publishers) 1999

LOOK, SAY, COVER	WRITE	CHECK
change		
children		
much		
such		
watch		

LOOK, SAY, COVER	WRITE	CHECK
high		
light		
might		
right		
birthday		
today		

LOOK, SAY, COVER	WRITE	CHECK
found		
round		
around		
sound		

LOOK, SAY, COVER	WRITE	CHECK
any		
baby		
every		
happy		
lady		
money		

LOOK, SAY, COVER	WRITE	CHECK
only		
suddenly		
first		
birthday		

LOOK, SAY, COVER	WRITE	CHECK
below	....	....
follow	....	....
show	....	....
window	....	....
yellow	....	....

LOOK, SAY, COVER	WRITE	CHECK
coming	....	....
does	....	....
money	....	....
mother	....	....
own	....	....
something	....	....

LOOK, SAY, COVER	WRITE	CHECK
walked	....	....
asked	....	....
jumped	....	....
opened	....	....
started	....	....
stopped	....	....
turned	....	....
used	....	....

LOOK, SAY, COVER	WRITE	CHECK
being	....	....
walking	....	....
coming	....	....
during	....	....
following	....	....
swimming	....	....
morning	....	....
something	....	....

© Stanley Thornes (Publishers) 1999

LOOK, SAY, COVER	WRITE	CHECK
woke	....	....
inside	....	....
place	....	....
those	....	....
while	....	....
white	....	....
write	....	....
blue	....	....
change	....	....

LOOK, SAY, COVER	WRITE	CHECK
between	....	....
green	....	....
goes	....	....
tries	....	....
eyes	....	....
near	....	....
year	....	....
heard	....	....

LOOK, SAY, COVER	WRITE	CHECK
often	....	....
children	....	....
garden	....	....
woken	....	....

LOOK, SAY, COVER	WRITE	CHECK
word	....	....
work	....	....
world	....	....
friend	....	....
gone	....	....
head	....	....
young	....	....

© Stanley Thornes (Publishers) 1999

LOOK, SAY, COVER	WRITE	CHECK
still	....	....
started	....	....
sister	....	....

LOOK, SAY, COVER	WRITE	CHECK
where	....	....
while	....	....
white	....	....
why	....	....
whole	....	....

LOOK, SAY, COVER	WRITE	CHECK
knew	....	....
know	....	....
whole	....	....
write	....	....

LOOK, SAY, COVER	WRITE	CHECK
birthday	....	....
inside	....	....
outside	....	....
something	....	....
today	....	....
without	....	....

LOOK, SAY, COVER	WRITE	CHECK
can't	....	....
didn't	....	....
don't	....	....
I'm	....	....

© Stanley Thornes (Publishers) 1999

name   date

Finish writing the letters of the alphabet.

a   b   c   d   e

Write the next letter of the alphabet.

st_   pq_   bc_

lm_   rs_   vw_

hi_   op_   mn_

Write the letter of the alphabet that comes between.

a_c   g_i   s_u

c_e   k_m   x_z

t_v   d_f   j_l

Write the letter of the alphabet that comes before.

_fg   _pq   _bc

_st   _lm   _ef

_rs   _kl   _qr

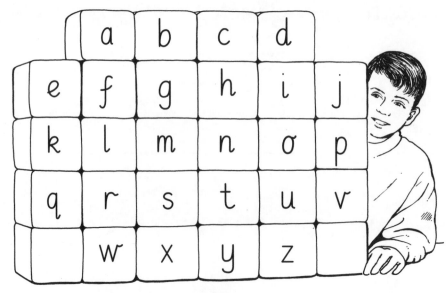

name _____   date _____

Look at the first letter of each word.

Write numbers in front of the words to show the alphabetical order. Then write the words in alphabetical order. The first box has been done for you.

a b c d e f g h i j k l m n o p q r s t u v w x y z

2 bat	1	_ant_
1 ant	2	_bat_
3 cat	3	_cat_

__ car	1	_____
__ dog	2	_____
__ egg	3	_____

__ fig	1	_____
__ hat	2	_____
__ goat	3	_____

__ pen	1	_____
__ oak	2	_____
__ nut	3	_____

__ ice	1	_____
__ hop	2	_____
__ goal	3	_____

__ rug	1	_____
__ sit	2	_____
__ quick	3	_____

name _____   date _____

Look at the first letter of each word.

Write numbers in front of the words to show the alphabetical order. Then write the words in alphabetical order. The first box has been done for you.

a b c d e f g h i j k l m n o p q r s t u v w x y z

3 park   1 _bark_

2 dark   2 _dark_

1 bark   3 _park_

---

3 rake   1 _____

1 cake   2 _____

2 lake   3 _____

__ wall   1 _____

__ ball   2 _____

__ tall   3 _____

__ pool   1 _____

__ tool   2 _____

__ fool   3 _____

__ beast   1 _____

__ least   2 _____

__ feast   3 _____

__ kiss   1 _____

__ miss   2 _____

__ hiss   3 _____

name _____ date _____

When the first letters of words are the same, you look at the second letter of each word.

Write numbers in front of the words to show the alphabetical order. Then write the words in alphabetical order. The first box has been done for you.

a b c d e f g h i j k l m n o p q r s t u v w x y z

3 hut   1 __hat__
2 hit   2 __hit__
1 hat   3 __hut__

___ goat   1 _____
___ game   2 _____
___ get   3 _____

1 wasp   1 _____
2 well   2 _____
3 when   3 _____

___ play   1 _____
___ pink   2 _____
___ pepper   3 _____

___ brake   1 _____
___ blast   2 _____
___ bunch   3 _____

___ men   1 _____
___ miss   2 _____
___ mask   3 _____

name _____   date _____

Number the words in each list in alphabetical order.

If two words begin with the same letter look at the second letters, and if the second letters are the same look at the third letters, and so on.

a b c d e f g h i j k l m n o p q r s t u v w x y z

opposites	_____	question	_____	capital	_____
vocabulary	_____	paragraph	_____	comma	_____
contractions	_____	sentence	_____	punctuation	_____
prefix	_____	statement	_____	abbreviation	_____
suffix	_____	command	_____	contraction	_____
homophones	_____	quote	_____	apostrophe	_____
antonyms	1	exclamation	_____	phrase	_____
synonyms	_____	subject	_____	chapter	_____

index	_____	adjective	_____	story	_____
accent	_____	noun	_____	novel	_____
definition	_____	adverb	_____	narrative	_____
pronounce	_____	pronoun	_____	poetry	_____
alphabet	_____	verb	_____	non-fiction	_____
dictionary	_____	tense	_____	letter	_____
titles	_____	possessive	_____	report	_____
spelling	_____	audience	_____	article	_____

name _____   date _____

In dictionaries, you will find guide words at the top of each page.
They show the first and last words on that page.

a b c d e f g h i j k l m n o p q r s t u v w x y z

Write whether these words come on the **bed – close** page, or on the
red – tooth page.

bee   _bed – close_   smell   _____

sleep   _____   rose   _____

blink   _____   catch   _____

referee _____   tame   _____

Write a word from the box that would be on the same page as each
pair of guide words.

arrow   water   planet   damp
wood   instrument   jelly   drink

ape – axe   _arrow_   doll – dry   _____

jar – just   _____   insect – island _____

cut – diver _____   wheat – wrong   _____

pine – price _____   wasp – wet   _____

name _____ date _____

Tick the words in each list that would be on the same page as the guide words.

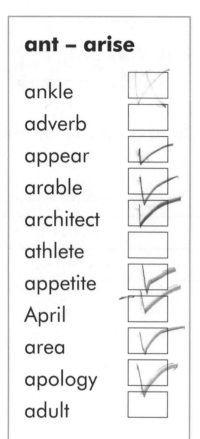

ant – arise

ankle	☑
adverb	☐
appear	☑
arable	☑
architect	☑
athlete	☐
appetite	☑
April	☑
area	☑
apology	☑
adult	☐

liquid – lord

lizard	☑
laugh	☒
list	☑
lark	☒
lofty	☑
lawn	☒
loot	☑
longitude	☑
lower	☑
lodge	☑
llama	☑

slink – snore

slunk	☑
smart	☒
shed	☒
snare	☑
sniff	☑
smoke	☑
sound	☑
stampede	☑
snivel	☒
slush	☑
slipway	☑

Write these two lists in alphabetical order. Then, at the top of each list, write the words that would be the guide words.

-------------- – --------------

hope	_____
huddle	_____
honey	_____
hour	_____
honest	_____
humbug	_____
homework	_____

-------------- – --------------

lace	_____
lather	_____
lawn	_____
lay	_____
larva	_____
last	_____
landing	_____

Key regular long vowel spellings

Learning targets

On completion of this section children will:

1 ➤➤ have thoroughly revised the spelling of words containing the long vowel phonemes

2 ➤➤ be able to 'hear' and 'read' the main vowel phonemes

3 ➤➤ have practised distinguishing between the different grapheme representations of the same phoneme (e.g. 'er', 'ur', 'ir') in their spelling.

Before you start

This section provides the opportunity to revise fully most of the work described in Section 5 (The long vowel phonemes) and Section 6 (Other common vowel phonemes) of *Learning Targets: Phonics and Spelling Key Stage* 1. It is inevitable, therefore, that there will be a considerable degree of overlap. As these are such important spelling families, the word lists are repeated for those without immediate access to the KS1 book, but all the photocopiable material in this book is different from the material the children might have encountered previously.

Background knowledge

Phonemes are the spoken form of the smallest sound units of words. Vowel phonemes can be represented by:

● digraphs (usually pairs of letters, e.g. '**roa**d')

● the so-called 'magic', or modifier, 'e' (e.g. 's**ide**')

● single letters (e.g. 'fl**y**').

Most common vowel phonemes are contained within regular and frequent letter clusters. They usually form the first sound in the rime pattern, so for most children it is easier to learn these patterns, whether decoding for reading, or encoding for writing, in their applied situation. It is, however, important to ensure that a thorough grounding is offered in the concept of a vowel digraph or similar vowel letter grapheme at the outset of the teaching process.

In *Learning Targets: Phonics and Spelling Key Stage* 1 the work focused mainly on teaching each digraph individually; at Key Stage 2 most pupils need to realise and appreciate that some sounds can be represented in several ways. The long 'a' vowel sound can, for example, be written as 'a' followed by a modifier 'e' as in 'game', 'ay' as in 'play', 'ai' as in 'train' and 'ei' as in 'eight'. (The last of these is covered in Section 4 Unit 17.)

Usha Goswami and others have shown that rhyme and analogy work with children can be important, not only in helping speed the reading process, but also in supporting spelling proficiency. Whilst blends and consonant digraphs, which were taught systematically in *Learning Targets: Phonics and Spelling Key Stage* 1, Sections 3 and 4, are most commonly associated with the onset part of the word, vowel phonemes are often integral to the rime part of the word, since the rime always carries the vowel sound. Being able to recognise rhyme leads children to appreciate that words comprise several units of sound, represented either by individual letters or by combinations of letters. Rhyme appreciation is thus important in teaching vowel digraphs as these are most frequently found in medial or final position in a word.

Rhyme also plays a significant role in the use of analogy in learning to spell well. Being able to spell the word 'room' for example, improves the chances of the child spelling 'broom' or 'spoon'.

Teaching the units

Units 1–11   Copymasters 8–18

This section comprises 11 units:

Unit 1:   **Long 'a'** (a–e; ai; ay)   (Copymaster 8)

Unit 2:   **Long 'e'** (ee; ea)   (Copymaster 9)

Unit 3:   **Long 'i'** (i–e; igh; y)   (Copymaster 10)

Unit 4:   **Long 'o'** (o–e; oa)   (Copymaster 11)

Unit 5:   **Long 'u'** (u–e; oo; ew) (Copymaster 12)

Unit 6:   **'ar'**   (Copymaster 13)

Unit 7:   **'air', 'are'**   (Copymaster 14)

Unit 8:   **'al', 'aw', 'or', 'au'**   (Copymaster 15)

Unit 9:   **'ir', 'ur', 'er'**   (Copymaster 16)

Unit 10: **'oi', 'oy'**   (Copymaster 17)

Unit 11: **'ou', 'ow'**   (Copymaster 18)

General teaching strategies

1   Ensure that there is a clear understanding of the distinction between 'short' and 'long' vowel sounds. Having revised what the five vowel letters are, remind the children that the short vowel sound is what the letter most simply represents (or 'says') and the long vowel is its 'name' (e.g. short 'a' in 'apple'; long vowel sound as in 'a, b, c, d, e …').

2   As with the long vowel digraphs, it can be helpful to point out that if two vowels appear in a syllable, usually the first is 'long' and the second is silent. Applying this to the modifier 'e', the effect can most graphically be represented by writing on the board five or six of the following words:

> win cub hat kit rob not tub tap plan fin cut hop pin can

Ask some children to read the words to the class. Point out that each of these words has only one vowel and that it therefore has a short sound. But if 'e' is added to the end of each of the words there are now two vowels. 'Magically' the first vowel in each case changes from short to long, while the second vowel (the 'e') remains silent.

3   Write two or three rhyming patterns on the board (e.g. 'ail', 'ain', 'ay'). Invite children to suggest rhyming words. The patterns that you select can be taken from the family word groups lists to ensure you select patterns for which there are a good number of words. Some of the words the children offer will rhyme but will have a different spelling pattern. Write these words nearby and use them as a discussion point. (With some individual children and groups it will be important to work on particular vowel digraphs individually, to ensure that they are fully mastered, before mixing them.)

Group or individual strategies

1   Use the copymasters as appropriate.

2   Write on the board words from general teaching strategy 2 above which you have not already used and invite the child or group to write the short and long vowel words, illustrate them and/or put the words in short sentences.

3   As an alternative to 2, write some gap sentences, offering the children the options of the short vowel and the long vowel words, e.g.

> I like that _____ . hat/hate

4   On the board write a number of your selected target words for a particular phoneme, omitting the digraph. The children should complete the words correctly, checking their spelling in a dictionary.

5   Have a few selected 'words of the week' for which the children find as many rhyming partner words as possible. These could be kept in folders or on display boards, and could possibly be linked to poetry writing activities from time to time.

Unit 1	Long 'a'

Useful family word groups

Simple long 'a' words	Long 'a' + blends, consonant digraphs
a-e (magic 'e')	
ape, ate	
bake, bale, base	blade, blame, blaze, brake, brave
cake, came, cane, cape, case, cave	crane, crate, chase
	flake, flame
gale, game, gate, gave, gaze	grape, grate, grave, graze
lake, lame, lane, laze	
made, make, male, mane, mate, maze	

safe, sake, sale, same, save

take, tale, tame, tape
wake, wave

ape, cape, tape,
ate, gate, mate,
bake, cake, lake, make, sake, take, wake
came, game, lame, same, tame
cave, gave, save, wave
made
base, case
bale, gale, male, sale, tale
gaze, laze, maze
cane, lane, mane

ace, face, lace, race
age, cage, page, rage, wage

plane, plate
slate, slave, skate, spade, stake, scale, snake, shade, shake, shave, shame, shape

grape, shape
crate, grate, plate, skate, slate
brake, flake, snake, stake, shake
blame, flame, shame
brave, grave, slave, shave
blade, spade, shade
chase
scale, whale
blaze, graze
crane, plane

place, grace, trace, space
stage

ai
aid, aim
maid, mail, main
paid, pail, pain
raid, rail, rain

aid, laid, maid, paid, raid
bail, fail, hail, jail, mail, nail
pail, rail, sail, tail, wail
main, pain, rain
sail, nail
rain
rail

frail, trail, snail
plain, stain, sprain, brain, drain, grain, train, chain
snail
train, strain, grain, brain, drain
frail, trail

ay (hay)
bay, day, hay, jay, lay, may
pay, ray, say, way
lay
ray
way
say

clay, play
bray, pray, tray, stray, spray
sway
stay

Related NLS sight words

said, April, again, came, made, make, take, name, may, way, day, away, play, May,

Sunday, Monday, Tuesday, Wednesday, Thursday, Friday, Saturday

Unit 2	Long 'e'

Useful family word groups

Simple long 'e' words	Long 'e' + blends, consonant digraphs

ee

bee, fee, see	free, tree
eel, feel, heel, peel, reel	steel
deed, feed, need, seed, weed	bleed, breed, greed, speed, tweed
been, keen, seen	green, screen
deep, jeep, keep, peep, seep, weep	sleep, creep, steep, sheep, cheep
feet, meet	fleet, sleet, tweet, sweet, sheet
leek, week	breeze, freeze, sneeze
see, seed, seek, seen, seem	
bee, beef, been	
fee, feel, feet	

ea

pea, sea, tea	flea
eat, beat, heat, meat, neat, peat, teat	bleat, treat, cheat
bean, lean, mean	clean
beam, seam, team	gleam, cream, dream, steam, scream, stream
deal, heal, meal, peal, seal, veal	steal
beak, leak, teak	freak, speak, sneak, tweak, streak
bead, lead, read	plead
heap, leap, reap	cheap
	bleach, preach
	each, beach, peach, reach, teach
	east, beast, feast, least, yeast
	heave, leave, weave
sea, seal, seam, seat	
tea, teak, team, teat	teach
pea, peal, peat, peak	peace
leaf, leak, lean, leap	

y

daddy, nanny
happy, nappy, ratty, tatty
very, merry, ferry, cherry
jelly, penny, teddy, smelly, messy
silly, chilly
dolly, lolly, lorry, poppy, foggy
rainy
easy, sleepy, leafy, creamy

'e'

be, he, me, we	she

Related NLS sight words

see, been, seen, tree, green, three

be, he, me, we, she, these, people

Unit 3	**Long 'i'**

Useful family word groups

Simple long 'i' words	Long 'i' + blends, consonant digraphs
i-e (magic 'e')	
bike, bite	
file, fine, five	
hide, hike, hive	
life, like, lime, line, live	
pike, pile, pine, pipe	
ride, ripe, rise	
side, site, size	
wide, wife, wine, wipe, wise	
bike, dike, hike, like, mike, pike	spike, strike
bite, kite, site	spite, sprite
dive, five, hive, jive, live	drive
file, mile, pile, tile, vile	stile, while, smile
fine, line, mine, nine, pine, vine, wine	spine, swine, twine, shine, shrine
hide, ride, side, tide, wide	glide, slide, bride, pride, stride
life, wife	
mime, time	crime, grime, prime, slime, chime
pipe, ripe, wipe	tripe, swipe, stripe
rise, wise	
size	prize
ice, dice, mice, nice, rice	slice, price, spice, twice, splice
die, lie, pie, tie	
y	
by, my, fly, sly, cry, dry, fry, try, sky	
spy, sty	
shy	
type, style	
igh	
high, sigh	thigh
fight, light, might, night, right, sight, tight	
light	blight, flight, slight
right	bright, fright

Related NLS sight words	time, like, live, white, by, my, night

Unit 4	**Long 'o'**

Useful family word groups

Simple long 'o' words	Long 'o' + blends, consonant digraphs
o-e	
code, coke, cone, cove	
dome, dope, doze	

hole, home, hope, hose
poke, pole, pope, pose
robe, rode, rope, rose

bone, cone, lone, tone, zone	stone, scone, throne
code, rode	strode
dope, hope, mope, pope, rope	slope, grope
dole, hole, mole, pole, role, vole	stole
home, coke, joke, poke, woke, yoke	broke, bloke, spoke, smoke, choke
hose, nose, pose, rose	close, prose, chose, those
note, tote, vote	drove
robe	globe, probe, froze

oe
doe, foe, hoe, toe

oa

oak, oat, coal, coat, coax	
load, loaf, loan	
soak, soap	
oat, boat, coat, goat, moat	float, throat, stoat, bloat
coal, foal, goal	shoal
foam, roam	
coax, hoax	
load, road, toad	
loan, moan	groan
oak	cloak, croak
	boast, coast, roast, toast
	coach, poach, roach

ow (snow)

bow, tow, sow, row, low, mow	show, throw, grow, snow
	blow, slow, flow, glow

Related NLS sight words

home, yellow

go, no, love, come, some, one, once

Unit 5	Long 'u'

Useful family word groups

Simple long 'u' words	Long 'u' + blends, consonant digraphs
u-e	
June, dune, tune	prune
lute, cute	flute, brute
duke	fluke
rule, yule	
use, fuse	
rude, nude	
cube, tube	

ue

cue, sue	blue, clue, glue, true

oo

boo, boom, boot	
hoof, hoop, hoot	
roof, room, root	
boo, moo, too, zoo	shoo
boom, doom, room, zoom	bloom, gloom, broom, groom
boot, coot, loot, hoot, root, toot	shoot, scoot
food, mood	brood
fool, pool, tool	spool, stool, school
hoof, roof	proof, spoof
hoop, loop	sloop, scoop, snoop, swoop, stoop, droop
moon, noon, soon	swoon, spoon, balloon
goose, loose, moose, noose	choose
booth, tooth	smooth

ew

yew, dew, few, mew, new	brew, crew, drew, grew
	stew, chew, threw, shrew
	blew, flew
	shrew, screw

'o'

do, to

Related NLS sight words

too, do (don't), new, blue, June
you, to, two, who, January, February, July

Unit 6	**'ar'**

Useful family word groups

Simple target words	**Target words with blends, consonant digraphs**
ar	
ark, arm, art	
bar, bark, barn	barge, large
car, card, cart	
dark, darn, dart	
hard, harm, harp	
bar, car, far, jar, tar	star, scar
ark, bark, dark, lark, mark, park	shark, spark
arm, farm, harm	charm
art, cart, dart, part, tart	start, smart, chart
barn, darn, yarn, card, hard, lard, yard	
harp, carp	sharp
	charge

harsh, marsh
arch, march

Related NLS sight words

are, March

after, half, last

Unit 7	Vowel phonemes 'are', 'air'

Useful family word groups

Simple target words	Target words with blends, consonant digraphs
are	
bare, care, dare, fare, hare, mare, rare	glare, spare, stare, scare, snare, share
air	
air, fair, hair, pair	flair, stair, chair

Related NLS sight words

are, there, their

Unit 8	'al', 'aw', 'au', 'or'

Useful family word groups

Simple target words	Target words with blends, consonant digraphs
al	
talk, walk	stalk, chalk
bald	scald
halt, malt, salt	
all, ball, call, fall, hall, tall, wall	small, stall
aw	
jaw, law, paw, raw, saw	claw, draw, thaw, straw
dawn, fawn, lawn, pawn, yawn	drawn, prawn, spawn
bawl	crawl, trawl, sprawl, shawl
hawk	
au	
cause, pause, because	clause
gauze	
	fault, vault
	haunt, daunt, flaunt
	launch

or

or, for
cord, ford, lord
cork, fork, pork   stork
form   storm
born, corn, horn, morn, torn, worn   sworn, shorn, scorn
fort, port, sort   snort, sport, short
gorge
force
gorse, horse, Morse
porch, torch, scorch
north
ore, bore, core, more, sore, tore, wore   store, score, snore, swore, shore

Related NLS sight words

all, ball, call, saw, or, for, more, door   *called, orange, laugh, because*

Unit 9	'ir', 'ur', 'er'

Useful family word groups

Simple target words	Target words with blends, consonant digraphs
ir	
fir, sir	stir
bird	third
dirt	flirt, skirt, shirt
firm	
girl	swirl, twirl
	first, thirst, chirp
	birth, mirth
ur	
urn, burn, turn	churn
fur	
curl, hurl	
hurt	
surf, turf	
urge, surge	
curse, nurse, purse	
curve	
	burnt, burst
	church
er	
her	
fern	stern
herb, kerb, verb	
herd	

jerk, perk
perm, term, germ
nerve, serve   swerve
verse

                                                       perch

Related NLS sight words
first, girl, her, were, over, sister, water   here, there, where, their

---

Unit 10	'oi', 'oy'

Useful 'oi' and 'oy' family word groups

Simple target words	Target words with blends, consonant digraphs
oi	
join	joint, joist
soil	spoil, spoilt
oil, boil, coil, soil, toil	spoil
coin, join	joint, point
	hoist, joist, moist
voice	choice
noise, poise	
oy	
boy, joy, toy	

Related NLS sight words   boy

Unit 11	**'ou', 'ow'**

Useful family word groups

Simple target words	Target words with blends, consonant digraphs
ou	
out, bout	
lout, pout, rout, tout	clout, trout, scout, spout, stout
	sprout, shout
foul	
loud	cloud, proud
noun	
house, louse, mouse	blouse, grouse, spouse
	bound, found, hound, mound, pound, round, sound, wound, ground
	count, fount, mount
ounce, bounce, pounce	flounce, trounce
lounge	scrounge
	couch, pouch, slouch, crouch
	mouth, south
ow	
bow, cow, how, now, row, sow	brow
owl, fowl, howl	growl, prowl, scowl
down, gown, town	clown, brown, crown, drown, frown
	crowd

Related NLS sight words

about, house, our, out, down, how, now	you, your, could, should, would, yellow

name _____ date _____

Sort the words into their spelling patterns and write them below.

rail came same sail
say play game stay tail
tame stray snail

ame words   **ail** words   **ay** words

_____   _____   _____

_____   _____   _____

_____   _____   _____

_____   _____   _____

Write two more words of your own to add to each list.

_____   _____   _____

_____   _____   _____

Choose words from the lists above to fill the gaps.

1 We found a little _____ kitten.

2 It had a fluffy _____ .

3 It _____ into our house.

4 It was very _____ .

5 "Look, it wants to _____ ," said Mum.

Sort the words into their spelling patterns and write them below.

bee each free sheep
tree keep beach sleep
deep teach reach see

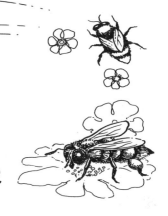

ee words

_____
_____
_____
_____

eep words

_____
_____
_____
_____

each words

_____
_____
_____
_____

Write two more words of your own to add to each list.

_____
_____

_____
_____

_____
_____

Choose words from the lists above to fill the gaps.

1 Gran took us to play on the _____.

2 She sat under a _____ out of the sun.

3 "Don't go in the _____ water!" said Gran.

4 "And swim where I can _____ you,"
   she said.

5 When we got back Gran had gone
   to _____.

name _____ date _____

Sort the words into their spelling patterns and write them below.

night like sky bike

shy hike might strike

light bright cry dry

ike words	**ight** words	**y** words
_____	_____	_____
_____	_____	_____
_____	_____	_____
_____	_____	_____

Write two more words of your own to add to each list.

_____	_____	_____
_____	_____	_____

Choose words from the lists above to fill the gaps.

1 It was a very dark _____.
2 "I don't _____ the dark," said my little brother.
3 "OK, I'll turn on the _____!" I said.
4 My little brother started to _____.
5 "Please don't cry; _____ your eyes."

name _____ date _____

Sort the words into their spelling patterns and write them below.

goat   joke   boat   float
roast   boast   smoke   broke   spoke
coast   coat   toast

oat words   **oast** words   **oke** words

_____   _____   _____

_____   _____   _____

_____   _____   _____

_____   _____   _____

Invent a made-up word of your own to add to each list.

_____   _____   _____

Choose words from the lists above to fill the gaps.

1 My favourite animal is my pet _____.

2 One day I was sure she _____ to me.

3 It made me drop her bottle, and it _____.

4 Mum was cross because the milk went all over my new
   _____.

5 When I told my dad he said it was a _____.

name _____ date _____

Sort the words into their spelling patterns and write them below.

blue stew soon clue noon true
glue chew moon threw spoon screw

ue words

_____

_____

_____

_____

oon words

_____

_____

_____

_____

ew words

_____

_____

_____

_____

Write a sentence to say what you notice about the letter patterns **ue** and **ew** in the words in the lists above.

_____

Choose words from the lists above to fill the gaps.

1   Grandad said he would tell me a _____ story.

2   One day he dropped a can of very sticky _____.

3   It fell in the _____ that Gran was cooking.

4   He said it made the meat stick to the _____.

5   Last week he told me he'd been to the _____!

name _____ date _____

Sort the words into their spelling patterns and write them below.

car dark start mark shark star
part smart spark far jar cart

ar words

_____
_____
_____
_____

ark words

_____
_____
_____
_____

art words

_____
_____
_____
_____

Write a sentence using two words from the lists above.

_____

What am I? You will find the words in the lists above.

1 I'm a large fish with sharp teeth. _____

2 I am the beginning of a race. _____

3 My hat is a tin lid that screws on. _____

4 I've one wheel inside and four outside. _____

5 I twinkle on a clear, dark night. _____

name _____ date _____

Hair and **care** rhyme, even though they have different endings.
Write four other words in each list that rhyme and have the
same endings.

hair _____

care _____

Find a matching word that ends in **air** or **are**.

1   two of a kind _____

2   very unusual _____

3   long steady look _____

4   grows on humans and animals _____

5   a female horse _____

6   similar to a rabbit _____

7   amusement park _____

8   a type of seat _____

9   the price of a journey _____

10 what we breathe _____

name _____ date _____

Sort the words into their spelling patterns and write them below.

fall thaw small straw saw
yawn call lawn draw horn torn
born worn stall dawn spawn

aw words	**awn** words	**orn** words	**all** words
_____	_____	_____	_____
_____	_____	_____	_____
_____	_____	_____	_____
_____	_____	_____	_____

Write two more words of your own to add to each list.

| _____ | _____ | _____ | _____ |
| _____ | _____ | _____ | _____ |

Write sentences that use each of these pairs of words.

1 horse _____

   corn _____

2 claw _____

   saw _____

3 talk _____

   walk _____

name   date

ir, **ur** and **er** often sound the same.

Use a dictionary to help you write the missing letters in these words.

1 d__ty   not clean

2 pict__e   a painting

3 swimm__   person who swims

4 sh__t   worn above the waist

5 n__se   works in a hospital

Make eight **ir** words using these two word wheels.

b   d   ___bird___
th   ir   d   _____
d   t   _____
sk   t   _____

sh   t   _____
b   ir   th   _____
f   st   _____
th   st   _____

Make a word wheel of your own for **ur** words.

___ ___   ___ ___   _____
     ur
___ ___   ___ ___   _____
___ ___   ___ ___   _____

name _____ date _____

Find a word from the box to match each picture.

Then find a second word that rhymes with each picture word.

Write both words underneath the picture.

> *coin   point   toy   oil*
> *boil   boy   join   joint*

_____   _____   _____   _____

_____   _____   _____   _____

Write sentences that use each of these pairs of words.

1 noisy _____

  voices _____

2 toy _____

  boy _____

3 join _____

  choice _____

Find and put a ring round the nine words hidden in this box that have the **out** spelling pattern.

s	n	a	a	b	o	u	t	r
o	s	p	r	o	u	t	r	a
s	s	h	o	u	t	p	o	o
s	t	o	u	t	m	e	u	s
l	c	t	s	c	o	u	t	u
c	l	o	u	t	q	u	o	n

Write two other words with the same spelling pattern as each of these words.

loud   _grouse_   _hound_

_____   _____   _____

_____   _____   _____

Write four more words in each of these lists that rhyme and have the same spelling pattern.

owl   _clown_

scowl   _frown_

_____   _____

_____   _____

_____   _____

Irregular, or variable, grapheme/phoneme relationships, including homophones

Learning targets

On completion of this section children will:

1 ➤➤ be aware of, and have practised, the more important homophones

2 ➤➤ have practised distinguishing between the different sound (phoneme) variations offered by some graphemes.

Before you start

Background knowledge

Phonemes are the spoken form of the smallest sound unit. Vowel phonemes can be represented by:

- digraphs (usually pairs of letters, e.g. 'r**oa**d')
- the so-called 'magic', or modifier, 'e' (e.g. 's**i**d**e**')
- single letters (e.g. 'fl**y**')

However, whilst a given sound can be represented in different ways (e.g. c**ow** and r**ou**nd, **ow** and **ou** both representing the same 'vowel phoneme'), equally the same letter grouping, or 'grapheme', can represent different vowel phonemes.

It is important to confront these potential confusions head-on and have an organised teaching strategy, and to this end the children should be helped to realise that there are various groupings:

- homophones, which are words that have the same sound (**homo** = 'same'; **phone** = 'sound') but different meaning and spelling (e.g. 'there' and 'their')
- homonyms, which are words with the same spelling pattern and sometimes the same sound but which have a different meaning (e.g. they **row** the boat; the old car made such a terrible **row**)
- other digraphs that can represent more than one sound (e.g. 'b**ea**d'; 'br**ea**d')

Teaching the units

Units 1–6   Copymasters 19–24

This part of the section comprises 6 units:

Unit 1: **'here'**, **'hear'**; **'to'**, **'too'**, **'two'** (Copymaster 19)

Unit 2: **'see'**, **'sea'**; **'right'**, **'write'** (Copymaster 20)

Unit 3: **'by'**, **'buy'**; **'blue'**, **'blew'** (Copymaster 21)

Unit 4: **'there'**, **'their'**, **'they're'** (Copymaster 22)

Unit 5: **More homophones 1** (Copymaster 23)

Unit 6: **More homophones 2** (Copymaster 24)

General teaching strategies

1 Write the following sentences on the board (without the underlines):

I <u>threw</u> the ball to my friend.

It went <u>through</u> the window!

Invite two children to read the sentences aloud. Ask if anyone can point to the two words that sound the same. Underline them. Invite definitions of the two words and stress that although they sound the same they have quite different meanings and spellings.

2 Ensure that there is a clear understanding of the meaning of 'homophone'. This will provide an opportunity to consider the origin of many English words, and especially the Greek derivation of this word.

3 Ask if anyone can offer other homophones, prompting as necessary from the list below. Write the pairs (or triplets) on the board. Invite the children in turn to offer short sentences that carry and demonstrate the meaning of the words.

Group or individual strategies

1 Use the copymasters as appropriate. A range is offered to enable you to pitch the work appropriately.

2 Write the following passage on the board.

Dad got a knew job last weak. He was scent to work on sum new houses. He was told to meat the foreman on the building sight. If he wasn't their he was told he should bee shore to weight until he arrived.

a) In discussion with the group, underline the homophones that are used incorrectly.

b) Rewrite the passage using the correct words.

3 Select a list of homophone words for the partner words to be identified. The two words should then, if possible, be combined within a single sentence. If this is too difficult the group/individual can write a separate sentence for each word.

4 There are many other opportunities for practising homophones, including when undertaking dictionary skills work.

5 As an ongoing activity, groups might compete to see who can collect the most homophones, or the class might collectively work on this, adding to a wall list whenever new sets are found.

Units 1–6	Some common homophones

Here is a selection of the more common homophones.

Note: Some of the following words, depending on dialect and accent, might not be pronounced with exactly the same sound, though in most cases they will be very close.

for, four	ball, bawl	not, knot	fir, fur
see, sea	by, buy, bye	no, know	tied, tide
way, weigh	sent, scent, cent	earn, urn	root, route
to, too, two	air, heir	meet, meat	some, sum
weather, whether	waste, waist	ate, eight	rode, road
there, their, they're	rows, rose	bread, bred	seller, cellar
peer, pier	straight, strait	horse, hoarse	current, currant
pour, poor	pray, prey	peal, peel	stationary, stationery
new, knew	medal, meddle	wood, would	stares, stairs
sale, sail	so, sow	knight, night	feet, feat
blue, blew	where, wear, ware	one, won	might, mite
bored, board	pair, pare, pear	seen, scene	more, moor
week, weak	or, ore, oar	hole, whole	our, hour
son, sun	saw, soar, sore	great, grate	flour, flower
steal, steel	isle, aisle	passed, past	ring, wring
pail, pale	plain, plane	missed, mist	bear, bare
hair, hare	groan, grown	threw, through	here, hear
cheep, cheap	rain, reign	you, ewe, yew	heal, heel
deer, dear	aloud, allowed	piece, peace	fort, fought
break, brake	right, write	rap, wrap	
male, mail	due, dew	heard, herd	

Units 7–15 Copymasters 25–33

This part of the section comprises 9 units:

Unit 7:	**'ea', 'ear'**	(Copymaster 25)
Unit 8:	**'y'**	(Copymaster 26)
Unit 9:	**'oo'**	(Copymaster 27)
Unit 10:	**Long 'a' (as in 'bath')**	(Copymaster 28)
Unit 11:	**'ire', 'ere', 'ure'**	(Copymaster 29)
Unit 12:	**'ild', 'ind'**	(Copymaster 30)
Unit 13:	**'ough'**	(Copymaster 31)
Unit 14:	**'ow'**	(Copymaster 32)
Unit 15:	**'o', 'u'**	(Copymaster 33)

General teaching strategies

1 Whenever teaching the 'irregular' grapheme/phoneme relationships, ensure the work is preceded by revision of the relevant regular form. Only when this is securely internalised should work begin on the variants.

2 Some children will have auditory difficulty in distinguishing some of the phonemes (e.g. 'ea' in 'year' and 'bread', or 'oo' in 'good' and 'food'). Lots of rhyme work can help.

3 Write headings on the board for each of the vowel sounds represented by a grapheme. Then write a list of 12–15 words containing the grapheme, split roughly equally between the different vowel sounds. Call on volunteers to choose a word, pronounce it, and circle the vowel digraph or relevant cluster. Then ask another child to copy the word under the heading that has the same vowel sound.

4 Divide the class into teams. Write a starter word on the board for each team (e.g. 'good' and 'boot'). The teams take it in turns to offer a word with the same phoneme and grapheme as their starter word.

5 Use groups of rhyming words to undertake shared poetry writing activities, focusing on simple rhyming couplets.

Group or individual strategies

1 Use the copymasters as appropriate.

2 Many of the activities on the copymasters are interchangeable between the various phoneme/grapheme relationships being taught.

3 Whenever possible devise ways of using and practising the words in a way that simultaneously reinforces another skill. For example, these patterns lend themselves to work on roots, suffixes and prefixes. Give each group or child a word, or two or three words, and ask them to create as many extended words as they can, e.g.

near: nearly nearby nearing neared.

4 As an ongoing activity, groups might compete to see who can collect the most examples of a given pattern, which makes good reading practice as well as providing spelling practice with some of the potentially more difficult words.

5 Offer pairs of words, one with a regular grapheme/phoneme relationship and the other with the variant. The challenge is to include both words in an amusing nonsense sentence.

Unit 7	'ea', 'ear'

Useful family word groups

See page 34 for pure 'ea' words (e.g. 'bead')

As in 'bread'
dead, head, read, lead
read, tread, thread, ready, already, spread, instead
feather, heather, leather, weather
health, wealth
measure, pleasure, treasure
deaf, breakfast, weapon, sweat, sweater, meadow, jealous, pleasant

As in 'ear'
year, hear, dear, fear, near, rear, clear, spear, beard

As in 'earl'
pearl, earn, learn, yearn, early, search, earth

As in 'bear'
pear, tear, swear

Unit 8   'y'

Useful family word groups

See page 35 for 'long y' words (e.g. 'fly')

There are numerous words, especially adjectives and adverbs, that end with 'y' making the 'ee' sound. Here are a few for reference. Notice how many also have a double consonant immediately before the 'y'.

daddy, nanny, nappy, happy
penny, teddy, berry, messy, smelly
lorry, dolly, hobby, poppy, dotty, foggy
lucky, mucky, dusty, rusty
baby, lady, lazy, crazy
rainy, brainy
easy, creaky, creamy, leafy, sleepy, cheeky

Unit 9   'oo'

Useful family word groups

See page 37 for pure 'oo' words (e.g. 'boot')

As in 'book'
cook, hook, look, rook, took, crook, brook, shook
foot, soot
good, hood, wood, stood
wool

Unit 10   Long 'a' (as in 'bath')

Useful family word groups

-ask
ask, bask, cask, mask, task, flask

-asp
gasp, rasp, clasp, grasp

-ast
cast, fast, last, mast, past, vast, blast, master

-ass
class, glass, brass, grass

-ant
plant, slant, grant, chant

-aff
staff

-ath
bath, path, lather, rather

-ance
dance, prance, chance

-anch
branch, ranch

Unit 11	'ire', 'ere', 'ure'

Useful family word groups

ere
here
there, therefore
where, wherever, nowhere, somewhere

ire
hire, mire, wire, sire, siren, shire, fire, fireman

ure
lure, cure, pure, nature, sure, measure, treasure, pleasure, creature, failure, picture, capture, puncture, furniture, pressure, future, pasture, insure, agriculture

Unit 12	'ild', 'ind'

Useful family word groups
-ild
mild, wild, child, godchild, grandchild

-ind
bind, find, kind, mind, wind, blind, grind, remind, unkind, behind

Unit 13	'ough'

Useful family word groups

As in 'off'
cough, trough

As in 'cuff'
rough, tough, enough

As in 'no'
dough, though

As in 'too'
through, throughout

As in 'fort'
ought, bought, fought, nought, sought, brought, thought, wrought

As in 'how'
bough, plough, slough, drought

As in 'sofa'
borough, thorough

Unit 14	'ow'

Useful family word groups

See page 41 for pure 'ow' words (e.g. 'cow')

As in 'rose'

bow, low, mow, row, sow, tow, bowl, own, sown, know, known
blow, blown, flow, flown, glow, slow, crow, grow, grown, stow, snow
show, shown
throw, thrown, growth
arrow, barrow, marrow, narrow
bellow, fellow, yellow, billow, pillow, willow
follow, hollow, shallow, swallow
burrow, furrow, sorrow, sparrow, tomorrow
widow, window, minnow, shadow, rainbow, hedgerow, elbow, crossbow

Unit 15	'o', 'u'

Useful family word groups

come, some, done, none, dove, love, glove, one, shove, above
other, mother, brother
money, monk, monkey, honey, front, frontier, smother
some, something, sometimes, somewhere
won, wonder, wonderful, worry

name _____ date _____

The words in the boxes are homophones.

Write the correct word in each gap.

| here hear | to too two |

Put the new speakers over _____.

I like to listen _____ music.

Can you _____ it from there?

Why do you need _____ speakers?

Can we play our CDs _____?

Gran said she could _____
the music from the end of our garden.

Mum has come in _____ dance.

Dad thinks he is a good dancer, _____.

Mum says he has _____ left feet!

Write your own sentences using the word in each box.

| here | _____ |
| hear | _____ |

name _____   date _____

The words in the boxes are homophones.

Write the correct word in each gap.

see sea	right write

I am going to _____ a letter to Gran.

I'll ask if we can go and _____ her.

I like visiting her because she lives near the _____ .

Her house is _____ next to the beach.

Last time we went the _____ was too rough for swimming.

Gran said I was _____ not to risk swimming.

I'd like to _____ Gran again.

I hope she'll _____ back soon.

Write your own sentences using the word in each box.

sea	_____
write	_____
right	_____

name .... date ....

The words in the boxes are homophones.

Write the correct word in each gap.

by buy

blue blew

I went to _____ a balloon.

My other one _____ away in the strong wind.

The balloon shop is _____ the bus stop.

I _____ it up on the way home.

Just as I was walking _____ our school I fell over.

The balloon burst, and all I had was a piece of _____ rubber.

I suppose I'll have to _____ another one!

Write your own sentences using the word in each box.

by _____

buy _____

name _____   date _____

The words in the box are homophones.

Write the correct word in each gap.

there   their   they're

We left our bikes over _____ by the tree.

The twins and I rode to _____ house.

_____ faster riders than me.

_____ mum was at home.

She said, "_____ is a lot of mess in your room.

Gran and Grandad have said _____ coming to stay, so please tidy up."

Write your own sentences using the word in each box.

| there | _____ |
| their | _____ |

name   date

Write a homophone for each word.

threw	_____	scent	_____
weak	_____	no	_____
there	_____	right	_____
heard	_____	stair	_____
pane	_____	flower	_____
peace	_____	soar	_____
meet	_____	rode	_____
heal	_____	grate	_____
by	_____	sum	_____
fought	_____	too	_____

Write sentences using the homophones in the boxes.
Try to use both words in the same sentence.

new knew	_____
	_____
eight ate	_____
	_____
where wear	_____
	_____

name _____   date _____

Write a homophone for each word.

knot _____   cent _____

aisle _____   sew _____

plain _____   break _____

coarse _____   bare _____

pain _____   strait _____

piece _____   him _____

sale _____   prey _____

grown _____   our _____

night _____   mite _____

rain _____   meddle _____

Write a definition of each of these homophones.
Use a dictionary to help you.

sail _____

sale _____

groan _____

grown _____

air _____

heir _____

knight _____

night _____

waste _____

waist _____

name _____   date _____

ea does not always make the same sound.

Read the words in the box, and write them in the correct list below.

hear   seat   tread   teacher   beat   head
year   spread   tear   each   deaf   nearer

ea as in **tea**   **ea** as in **ear**   **ea** as in **bread**

_____   _____   _____
_____   _____   _____
_____   _____   _____
_____   _____   _____

Now write two more of your own words to add to each list.

_____   _____   _____
_____   _____   _____

Write the answer to each of these clues. Each one has an **ear** or **ead** spelling pattern.

1   The top part of your body, beginning with h _____

2   Another word for 'close', beginning with n _____

3   Falls from your eye when you're upset, beginning with t _____

4   Sandwiches would be impossible without it, beginning with b

_____

5   You have two on your head, beginning with e _____

6   Twelve months makes one of these, beginning with y _____

name _____ date _____

y on the end of a word does not always make the same sound.

Read the words in the box, and write them in their correct list below.

happy fly merry cry puppy
spy try floppy shy silly

y as in **my**

_____

_____

_____

_____

y as in **nappy**

_____

_____

_____

_____

Now add two more of your own words to each list.

_____

_____

_____

_____

The answer to each of these clues is a word that ends with **y** that sounds like 'ee'.

1 The opposite of 'clean', beginning with d _____

2 Another word for 'cheerful', beginning with h _____

3 The opposite of 'difficult', beginning with e _____

4 The taste of sea water, beginning with s _____

5 A fire with lots of smoke, beginning with s _____

name _____   date _____

oo doesn't always make the same sound.

Read the words in the box, and write them in their correct list below.

| door shook shoot moor spoon |
| look groom floor took crook broom |

oo as in **room**   **oo** as in **book**   **oo** as in **poor**

_____   _____   _____

_____   _____   _____

_____   _____   _____

_____   _____

Now write two more of your own words to add to each
of the first two lists.

_____   _____

_____   _____

The answer to each of these clues is an **ook** spelling pattern word.

1 Hangs on the end of a fishing line, beginning with h _____

2 A name for a burglar, beginning with C _____

3 Someone who works in a kitchen, beginning with C _____

4 We do this with our eyes, beginning with l _____

5 A large black bird, beginning with r _____

6 It has pages, words and pictures, beginning with b _____

name _____ date _____

ar is a common spelling pattern,

　　e.g.　p**ar**k　b**ar**king

Sometimes **a** by itself can make the sound of **ar**,

　　e.g.　**a**sk　p**a**st　p**a**ss

Circle the odd-word-out in these groups, and write the main spelling pattern in each set.

ask	flask	mask	(mark)	task	_ask_
fast	last	shark	master	blast	_____
pass	brass	grass	class	cart	_____
craft	draft	dart	shaft	after	_____
plant	slant	grant	smart	chant	_____
bath	barter	path	rather	lather	_____
dance	prance	chance	sharp	lance	_____

One of the words from each of the above groups is the answer to each of these clues.

1　A container for liquid, beginning with f　　_flask_

2　Very quick, beginning with f　　_____

3　A yellowish metal, beginning with b　　_____

4　Antonym for 'before', beginning with a　　_____

5　Slope, beginning with S　　_____

6　A large container for water, beginning with b　　_____

7　An opportunity, beginning with C　　_____

name   date

ir, **ur** and **er** often sound the same, but **ire**, **ure** and **ere** do not.

Complete the **ire**, **ure** or **ere** word to match each definition.

1 f _____ flames

2 h _____ opposite of there

3 s _____ certain

4 h _____ pay to use

5 w _____ long metal thread

Hidden in this puzzle are words that have either the **ire** or **ure** spelling pattern. Copy the words in the correct box, then add some more of your own. When you have finished, tick the box with the most words.

g	d	c	e	p	f	m	l
n	q	s	h	i	r	e	r
p	j	b	k	c	u	r	e
o	a	n	a	t	u	r	e
m	e	a	s	u	r	e	v
f	u	t	u	r	e	h	i
t	s	u	r	e	s	w	u

ure words	**ire** words

Write a sentence using the words **sure** and **shore**.

_____

_____

name _____ date _____

In the spelling patterns **ild** and **ind**, **i** usually sounds like the **i** in **kite**.
Copy the short **ild** or **ind** word that is in each of the long words.

minder	*mind*	unkind	_____
unwind	_____	minding	_____
rewinding	_____	blindingly	_____
kindness	_____	grinding	_____
childless	_____	unkindly	_____
children	_____	childish	_____
wildly	_____	wilderness	_____

How are **children** and **wilderness** different from the other words?

_____

If **child** is the 'root word' of **children**, write the root words for these words.

minder	*mind*	unkind	_____
unwind	_____	minding	_____
rewinding	_____	blindingly	_____
kindness	_____	grinding	_____
childless	_____	unkindly	_____
children	_____	childish	_____
wildly	_____	wilderness	_____

Write a sentence using the words **wind** (the weather) and **wind** (to wind up).

_____

The **ough** spelling pattern can have several sounds. Find two words from the list to rhyme with the letters underlined in each box.

through
trough
rough
cough
bough
borough
fought
throughout
bought
dough
thorough
enough
though
plough

o<u>ff</u>	p<u>uff</u>
s<u>o</u>	b<u>oo</u>
s<u>ort</u>	c<u>ow</u>
sof<u>a</u>	

Use a dictionary to find the meaning of each of these words.

doe   _____

dough   _____

threw   _____

through   _____

bow   _____

bough   _____

fort   _____

fought   _____

ruff   _____

rough   _____

name _____ date _____

ow doesn't always make the same sound.

Read the words in the box, and write them in their correct list below.

down flow clown window how
snow owl grow growl follow

ow as in **town**

_____

_____

_____

_____

_____

ow as in **crow**

_____

_____

_____

_____

_____

Now write two more of your own words to add to each list.

_____   _____

_____   _____

The answer to each of these clues is a word that ends with **ow**.

1 The opposite of 'high', beginning with l   _____

2 White flakes that fall from the sky, beginning with S   _____

3 A special knot in a ribbon, beginning with b   _____

4 What we do with seeds, beginning with S   _____

5 We use oars to do this in a boat, beginning with r   _____

name   date

o can often sound the same as **u** in b**u**tter.

Each of these words has a missing **u** or **o**. Write in the correct letter, then use a dictionary to check your answers.

m__ney	s__me	br__ther
__ther	n__ne	fr__nt
c__me	s__nny	m__nkey
m__ddy	n__n	sm__ther
m__ther	g__tter	h__nter
h__ney	m__nk	s__mething

We sometimes muddle **full** and **fool**. This is because **ull** sounds similar to **ool** and **all**. Put each of these words in sentences to show you know what they mean.

pull   _____

pool   _____

full   _____

fool   _____

bull   _____

ball   _____

Other significant clusters/strings

Learning targets

On completion of this section children will:

1 ➼ have revisited and revised the spelling of words containing the main blends and clusters
2 ➼ have revised the consonant digraphs
3 ➼ have become aware of some of the more significant word endings
4 ➼ have been helped to appreciate the difference between and reasons for the occurrence of soft and hard 'c' and 'g'.

Before you start

This section provides the opportunity to revisit the work on blends in Section 3 (Significant consonant blends and end clusters) and Section 4 (Consonant digraphs) of *Learning Targets: Phonics and Spelling Key Stage* 1. It is inevitable, therefore, that there will be a degree of overlap, but here the work in the earlier book is covered in far greater detail and with more differentiation. Here, these important groupings are brought together and presented in a more integrated and comparative way. For some, especially the less able, younger children, it is suggested that some of the earlier book's copymasters might be more appropriate. However, if you do not have immediate access to the Key Stage 1 book the word lists are repeated, but all the photocopiable material in this book is different from the material the children might have encountered previously.

Background knowledge

Blending is the smooth running together of two or more individual sounds, usually consonants, such as '**bl**ot', '**pr**am', '**str**ap', 'sa**nd**'. Blends most commonly occur at the beginning or end of a word, and are sometimes referred to as 'initial blends' and 'final blends'. The blend can form the entire onset of the word or syllable. As such they are important when the child is making analogies between similar sounding words, e.g. being able to hear the 'str' in 'strip' makes it easier to spell if the child is already able to read and spell 'strap'.

Blends and clusters should not be confused with digraphs. Digraphs are groups (usually pairs) of letters, either consonants or vowels or one of each (e.g. 'sh', 'ea' and 'eer'), which operate together to represent a single sound, such as '**sh**op', 'h**ea**t' and 'd**eer**').

Consonant digraphs are those which represent a consonant sound. The most significant, and the one most readily recognised by early readers and writers, is 'sh'. It is found in many words, either in an initial position or in a final position. The digraph 'th' is more difficult for some children, especially as it is pronounced in two ways (as in '**th**ink', with the tongue pushed forward between the teeth, or as in '**th**at') and is technically two different consonant sounds. But it is an important grapheme, occurring as it does in many of the high-frequency sight recognition words.

Consonant digraphs become a useful prop when the child is making analogies between similar sounding words. It is helpful to be aware that, with a few exceptions, 'ch' in the final position in a word is nearly always separated from the preceding vowel by either an 'n' or a 't'. (e.g. 'lunch', 'catch').

Teaching the units

Units 1–21   Copymasters 34–54

This section covers 21 units:

Unit 1:   **Final 'ck'**   (Copymaster 34)

Unit 2:   **Consonant digraph 'ng'**   (Copymaster 35)

Unit 3:   **Consonant digraph 'nk'**   (Copymaster 36)

Unit 4:   **Initial 'l' blends**   (Copymaster 37)

Unit 5:   **Initial 'r' blends**   (Copymaster 38)

Unit 6:   **Initial 's' blends**   (Copymaster 39)

Unit 7:   **Consonant digraphs 'sh', 'ch'**(Copymaster 40)

Unit 8:   **Consonant digraphs 'th', 'wh'**(Copymaster 41)

Unit 9:   **Letter strings '-tch', '-nch'**   (Copymaster 42)

Unit 10: **Simple double consonants**   (Copymaster 43)

Unit 11: **'et' endings**   (Copymaster 44)

Unit 12: **Digraph 'qu'**   (Copymaster 45)

Unit 13: **Digraph 'wa'**   (Copymaster 46)

Unit 14: **Soft 'c'**   (Copymaster 47)

Unit 15: **Soft 'g'**   (Copymaster 48)

Unit 16: **Letter string 'dge'**   (Copymaster 49)

Unit 17: **Digraphs 'ie', 'ei'**   (Copymaster 50)

Unit 18: **'al', 'el', 'le' endings**   (Copymaster 51)

Unit 19: **'en', 'on' endings**   (Copymaster 52)

Unit 20: **'ar', 'er', 'or' endings**   (Copymaster 53)

Unit 21: **'y', 'ey' endings**   (Copymaster 54)

General teaching strategies

1   The first six units practise the basic concept of word building for those children who still require such guidance. A useful way of achieving this is by vowel substitution. Depending on the target cluster, put a list of words on the board and invite children to make other words, simply by changing the vowel letters, e.g.

pack peck pick puck

This also helps to reinforce the notion of 'vowels'.

2   A variation on 1 above is to see how many words can be built by changing the onset. This brings in the possibility of revising consonant digraphs as well as single letters or blends, e.g.

pack tack track shack

3   A useful way to organise a whole class session on word endings is to write on the board a short piece of text with incorrect word endings. Invite volunteers to spot the deliberate mistakes, and to correct them on the board.

4   When introducing the concept of soft 'c' or 'g', write a list of words on the board, with either soft or hard letters, and a few with both. Read them slowly and deliberately, asking the children to raise their hands when the word contains a soft letter. As the soft and hard letters are identified write them in separate lists. From these lists it will be possible to demonstrate that, with some exceptions, 'c' or 'g' is soft when it comes immediately before 'e', 'i' or 'y' and hard before the vowels 'a', 'o' or 'u' or any consonant.

Group or individual strategies

1   Use the copymasters as appropriate.

2   Although covered elsewhere in this programme, the early units in this section can be used for work on inflectional endings. For example, give groups lists of words to incorporate in sentences. Then ask the children to rewrite each sentence as though it happened yesterday (past tense).

3   Similarly, plurals can be practised alongside many of these units, especially as they give an excellent opportunity to demonstrate the rule about adding 'es' to words ending with 'sh', 'ch', 's' or 'x', and the rule relating to changing the final 'y' to 'i' before adding 'es'.

4   Group or individual work on word endings might include offering the children groups of words that have the same ending, with their endings omitted, so that they can work them out.

5   When teaching soft 'c' or 'g' words, write on the board a list of words that are covered by the rule described in General teaching strategies paragraph 4 (above). For each word write an equivalent that is misspelt, though phonetically correct, e.g. 'tragedy'/'trajedy'; 'reject'/'regect', 'rejoice'/'regoice'. The children should use their dictionaries to choose the correct spelling, and where possible explain how the correct spelling fits with the rule.

Unit 1   Final 'ck'

Useful family word groups

Final 'ck'	Initial blend + final 'ck'
back, lack, pack, rack, sack, tack	black, crack, track, stack, smack, snack, quack, shack
deck, neck, peck	speck, check
kick, lick, pick, sick, tick, wick	click, flick, slick, brick, trick, stick, quick, chick, thick
dock, lock, rock, sock	block, clock, flock, frock, stock, smock, chock
duck, luck, muck, suck, tuck	cluck, pluck, truck, stuck, struck, chuck

Related NLS sight words

back, black

Note: final 'ck' is rarely found in association with long vowels, and the 'k' sound after a short vowel is almost always spelt 'ck' (except in multi-syllable words ending in 'ic', e.g. 'terrific').

Unit 2   Consonant digraph 'ng'

Useful family word groups

Final 'ng'	Initial blend + final 'ng'
bang, fang, gang, hang, rang sang, tang	clang, twang, sprang
ding, king, ping, ring, sing wing, zing	cling, fling, sling, swing, spring bring, sting, string
dong, gong, long, pong, song	prong, strong
dung, hung, lung, rung, sung	clung, flung, slung, stung, swung, sprung, strung

Related NLS sight word

going

Unit 3   Consonant digraph 'nk'

Useful family word groups

Final 'nk'	Initial blend + final 'nk'
bank, rank, sank, tank	blank, clank, crank, drank, plank, prank, spank
ink, link, mink, pink, rink sink, wink	blink, clink, drink
bunk, junk, sunk	clunk, drunk, trunk

Unit 4	Initial 'l' blends

Useful family word groups

	Initial 'l' blends	Initial 'l' blends + final blends/digraphs
bl-	blade, blame, blaze bled, bleed, blew blob, blot, blow blue	blank blink blush
cl-	clan, clap, claim clip clog, clot, close, cloak, cloud club	clash cling
fl-	flag, flan, flap, flat, flake, flame fleet flip flog, flop	flash flesh flush
gl-	glad glide glum, glue	
pl-	plan, plate, plane, plain plod, plop, plot plug, plum, plus	plank
sl-	slab, slam, slap slid, slim, slip, slit, slide slot slug, slum	slung, slush

Unit 5	Initial 'r' blends

Useful family word groups

	Initial 'r' blends	Initial 'r' blends + final blends/digraphs
br-	brake, brave, brain bright broke, brook, brown	bring brush
cr-	crab, crag, cram, crate creek, cream crib, crime crop	crank, crash
dr-	drab, drag, dram, drain, draw dream drip, drive drop drug, drum	drank

fr-	free fright frog, from	fresh	
gr-	grab, Gran, grape green grid, grim, grin, grip, grit grog grub	grand grunt	
pr-	pram prep prop	 print	
tr-	tram, trap, train tree trim, trip trod, trot	tramp trunk, trust	

Unit 6   Initial 's' blends

Useful family word groups

	Initial 's' blends	Initial 's' blends + final blends /digraphs	Three letter blends
scr-			scram, scrap, scrub, scrum
sk-	skate, skid, skim, skin, skip	skirt, skunk	
sm-		smack	
sn-	snap, snake, snail, snare snip snob snug		
sp-	span, spat, spade, spear, speed, spin, spit, spike, spine, spot, spoon spun	 spend, spent sport	
spl-			split, splint
spr-			sprint
st-	stab, stag, stale, stay, stain, stairs steal, steam, steel stem, step, stew stole, stool, stop stub, stun	stamp, stand stilts, sting storm stumps, stunt, stung	strap
str-			strip
sw-	swam swig, swim		

78

swop
swum

Unit 7	Consonant digraphs 'sh', 'ch'

Useful family word groups

ch-

chap, chat, chase, chain, chalk, charm, chart, chair
chest, check, chess, cheese, cheap, cheat
chin, chip, chit, chill, chick, chimp, chirp, chime
chop, choose
chug, chum, chuck, chunk, church, churn

-ch

each, beach, peach, reach, teach, bleach, preach
coach, poach, porch, torch, arch, perch, couch
rich
much, such

Related NLS sight words

much, March

Useful family word groups

sh-	**shr-**
sham, shall, shack, shade, shake, shame, shape, shave, sharp, share	shrank
shed, shelf, shell, sheet	shred
shin, ship, shift, shine, shirt	shrimp, shrink
shop, shot, shock, shoot, shook, short, shout	
shut	shrunk

-sh

ash, bash, cash, dash, gash, lash, mash,
rash, sash
mesh
dish, fish, wish
cosh, posh
hush, rush
clash, flash, slash, crash, smash, splash
flesh, fresh
swish
splosh
blush, flush, plush, slush, brush, crush

Related NLS sight words

push, should

Unit 8	Consonant digraphs 'th', 'wh'

th-	than, that them, then this	thank thin, thing, think, thick, thrill throb, three, throne, throat thud, thumb, thump, thrust	**Related NLS sight words** than, that, them, then, this, with their, there, these, three, they, brother, another
-th	with bathe smooth	depth fifth, sixth, tenth, width moth, cloth bath, teeth, tooth, north, south, mouth, birth	
wh-	whack, whale when, wheat, wheel, where whiz, whisk, which, whisky, whisker, whistle, while, whine, whirl who, whose, whole why		**Related NLS sight words** when what, where, who, white (-ite magic 'e')

Unit 9	Letter strings 'tch', 'nch'

Useful family word groups

-tch	-nch
batch, catch, hatch, match, patch, snatch, scratch fetch, sketch, stretch itch, bitch, ditch, hitch, pitch, witch, stitch, switch hutch, crutch	 bench, drench, trench finch, pinch bunch, lunch, munch, punch

Unit 10	Simple double consonants

Useful family word groups

	Double consonants	Blends + double consonants
-ff	biff buff, cuff, huff, puff	cliff, stiff, sniff fluff, gruff, stuff
-ll	bell, fell, sell, tell, well, yell ill, bill, fill, hill, kill, mill pill, till, will	spell, smell, swell drill, frill, grill, skill, spill, still swill

	doll	
	gull, hull	skull

-ss	ass, lass, mass	
	less, mess	bless, dress, press, stress
	hiss, kiss, miss	
	boss, moss, toss	floss, gloss, cross
	fuss	

Related NLS sight words

off, will, all, call, pull

Unit 11	**'et' endings**

Useful family word groups

magnet, tablet, jacket, packet, racket, gadget, blanket, cabinet
helmet, velvet, pellet
piglet, fillet, ticket, wicket, cricket, triplet, thicket
bonnet, locket, pocket, rocket, socket
upset, bullet, puppet, bucket, trumpet

Unit 12	**Digraph 'qu'**

Useful family word groups

quack
quell, quench, question, banquet, conquest
quit, quiz, quill, quilt, quick, squint, squirrel, liquid
quake
quaint
queen, squeeze
squeak
quite
squaw, squall
square

Unit 13	**Digraph 'wa'**

Useful family word groups

was, wasp
wand, want
wash
watch, swatch
war, ward, warm, warn

water
swan, swap, swamp

Unit 14   Soft 'c'

Useful family word groups

cell, cent
cease
cedar, cellar, cement, centre, central, ceiling, certain, centaur
celery, cereal, century, certify, celebrate, centipede
cemetery, centurion, ceremony, certificate
recent, accept, excel, except, cancel
excess, exceed, process, proceed, success
succeed, grocer, concert
December, excellent, innocent
ace, face, lace, pace, race
ice, dice, mice, nice, rice, slice, price, spice, twice, splice
notice, office, police, service
truce, spruce, puce
peace
city, civic, civil, cider, cigar
cinder, circus, circuit, circle, citrus
cigarette, cinema, circular, citizen, civilian
acid, pencil, icing, decide
accident, ferocity, electricity, simplicity
cycle, cyclone, Cyclops, cymbal, cygnet, cynic, cylinder
icy, lacy, fancy, juicy
spicy, agency, currency, frequency, conspiracy
dance, lance, fence, pence, mince, since, wince
ounce, bounce, pounce
glance, prance, trance, chance, prince
advance, distance, entrance, finance, absence, commence, defence, offence, sentence, convince, announce

Unit 15   Soft 'g'

Useful family word groups

gem, genie, germ, gentle, gesture, general, generous, genuine, geography, geometry
agent, angel, urgent, danger, larger, manager, stranger
digestion, emergency, vegetable, tragedy
age, cage, page, rage, sage, wage
huge
gin, giblet, giant, giraffe, ginger, gibberish
agile, legion, region, margin, magic, tragic
original, legible, regiment, energy, magistrate

gym, gypsy, gyroscope, gymnastics
range, arrange, change, grange, exchange, orange, strange, challenge, revenge, scavenge, fringe,
hinge, twinge, syringe, sponge, plunge
(See also **dge** endings in Unit 16)

Unit 16	Letter string 'dge'

Useful family word groups

badge, badger, cadge
edge, hedge, ledge
ridge, bridge, fridge
dodge, lodge, lodger
fudge, judge, nudge

Unit 17	Digraphs 'ie', 'ei'

Useful family word groups

ie (piece)

niece, piece, siege
brief, grief
priest, frieze
shield, chief, thief, shriek
belief, believe, relief, relieve

ie (friend)

friend

ie (view)

view, review

ei (height)

height
either, neither
eiderdown

ei (leisure)

leisure

ei (rein)

rein, veil, vein
feint
reign, beige
neigh, weigh, eight, weight
sleigh, freight
eighty, eighteen, eightieth, neighbour

Unit 18   'al', 'el', 'le' endings

Useful family word groups

-al

sandal, vandal, capital, classical, natural, national, factual
medal, metal, pedal, petal, dental, medical, central, mechanical
signal, historical, accidental, bridal
coral, comical, topical, tropical, hospital, horizontal
musical

-el

camel, panel, barrel, pastel, flannel, gravel, travel, cancel
channel, chapel, satchel
caramel, mackerel
kennel, vessel, kestrel
tinsel, swivel, minstrel, shrivel, chisel
hovel, novel, grovel, mongrel, hostel, cockerel
duffel, funnel, tunnel, mussel

-le

bramble, scramble, tremble, nimble, thimble, humble, jumble, grumble, stumble
temple, dimple, pimple, simple
candle, handle, swindle, bundle
angle, bangle, dangle, jangle, tangle, spangle, strangle, rectangle
jingle, mingle, single, tingle, bungle, jungle
ankle, rankle, tinkle, winkle, crinkle, twinkle, sprinkle
nestle, trestle, bristle, gristle, thistle, jostle, bustle, hustle, rustle

Unit 19   'en', 'on' endings

Useful family word groups

-en

batten, fatten, flatten, bitten, kitten, mitten, rotten
happen, sudden
dampen
seven, heaven, given, siren, golden, soften, wooden, oxygen
sunken, burden

-on

cotton, button, mutton, glutton
lesson, reckon, ribbon, common
sermon, lemon, bacon, matron, pardon, iron
skeleton, squadron
piston, prison, person, reason, season

Unit 20	'ar', 'er', 'or' endings

Useful family word groups

-er

enter, conquer, gather, deliver, discover, suffer, upper, clever, after, altogether, powder, corner, shower, register, weather, winter, letter, computer, quarter, drawer, water, newspaper, September

-or

motor, radiator, indicator, transistor, anchor, mirror, corridor, reactor, error, junior, interior, superior

-ar

altar, calendar, grammar, beggar, vinegar, burglar, cellar, regular, popular, singular, peculiar, familiar, circular, similar

Unit 21	'y', 'ey' endings

Useful family word groups

-y

by, my, fly, sly, cry, dry, fry, try, sky, spy, sty, shy
Daddy, nanny, nappy, tabby, tatty, Granny
jelly, jetty, penny, berry, cherry
hobby, holly, lorry, poppy
buggy, dummy, Mummy, puppy
baby, lady, gravy, daisy, ivy, posy, story, county, daily

-ey

abbey, alley, valley, volley, donkey, monkey, honey, hockey, jockey, dopey
trolley, pricey, chimney, chutney, barley, turkey, journey

name _____ date _____

Add an **a**, **e** or **i** to these words.
Then write a sentence using each word.

p_ck _____

p_ck _____

p_ck _____

Make these words.

b
p — ack   back _____
s

p
n — eck   _____
d

t
p — ick   _____
s

r
l — ock   _____
s

name _____   date _____

Add an **a**, **i** or **o** to these words.

Then write a sentence using each word.

s_ng _____

s_ng _____

s_ng _____

Make these words.

b
g ─ ang   <u>bang</u>
s   _____

                 _____

k
r ── ing   _____
p
                 _____

l
p ── ong   _____
s
                 _____

r
l ── ung   _____
b
                 _____

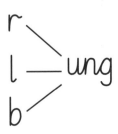

name _____   date _____

Add an **a**, **i** or **u** to these words.

Then write a sentence using each word.

s_nk _____

s_nk _____

s_nk _____

Make these words.

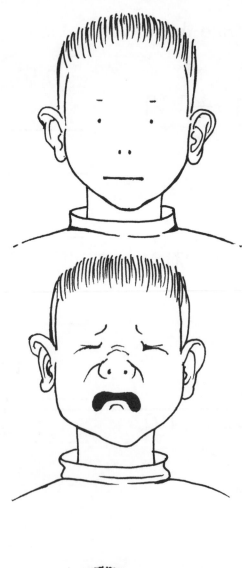

bl
th —ank   blank _____
s

st
shr —ink   _____
p   _____

shr
dr —unk   _____
b   _____

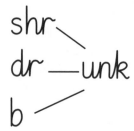

name _____ date _____

Write a word on each brick.

Make the words by joining a beginning to an end.

One is done to help you.

Beginnings	**Ends**
fl pl sl	ing uck ick ot
bl cl gl	op um ank

fl + ing
fling

Invent a meaning for this nonsense word.

glick	_____

Invent two words and meanings of your own.

	_____
	_____

name _____ date _____

Write a word on each brick.

Make the words by joining a beginning to an end.

One is done to help you.

Beginnings

cr dr fr br
gr pr tr

Ends

ip ush uck ick ess
um ill op ing

dr + ip
drip

Invent a meaning for this nonsense word.

gruck _____

Invent two words and meanings of your own.

☐ _____

☐ _____

name .... date ....

Write a word on each brick.

Make the words by joining a beginning to an end.

One is done to help you.

Beginnings

st str
sp spr spl

Ends

ing uck ick ess
it um ill

str + um
strum

Invent a meaning for this nonsense word.

splum _____

Invent two words and meanings of your own.

_____

_____

Add **sh** or **ch** to finish the words in the box.

__op __ips __in __ick __art __ell
__all __ed __ut __elf __ock

Now sort them into two lists.

sh words

ch words

Finish these words so that they match the clues by adding **sh** or **ch**.

1 ri__   has a lot of money

2 di__   a type of bowl

3 fla__   sudden bright light

4 fi__ing   a popular hobby

5 fin__   a small bird

6 bru__   used for sweeping

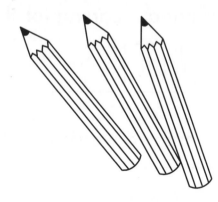

Add **th** or **wh** to finish the words in the box.

__in __ich __ink __ick __ere __at
__en __em __an __y __ite __ale

Now sort them into two lists.

th words   **wh** words

Finish these words so that they match the clues by adding **th** or **wh**.

1 __in   opposite of thick

2 mo__   attracted to lights at night

3 __eel   a bike has two

4 __eat   is ground to make flour

5 four__   immediately before fifth

6 __en   a question word about time

name Jody   date 16.11.06

When **ch** appears in the middle or at the end of a word it usually has a **t** or **n** in front of it.

Example: ma**t**ch   mu**n**ch   mu**n**ching

Write the missing letter in each of these words.
For one word you can use either **t** or **n**.

hi_ch   lu_ch   be_ch

fi_ch   ca_ch   fe_ch

pu_ching   swi_ched   stre_ching

wi_ches   bewi_ched   bu_cher

Find nine words ending in **tch** or **nch** that are hidden in this puzzle.

a	c	f	i	n	c	h	p
s	k	e	t	c	h	a	c
h	u	t	c	h	a	t	h
b	l	c	h	a	n	c	e
f	i	h	i	e	g	h	c
c	h	o	p	a	e	b	k

_____   _____   _____

_____   _____   _____

_____   _____   _____

name _____ date _____

Some letters often come together in pairs. Choose **ss**, **ll**, **ff** or **tt** to finish these words.

o__ te__ fi__ dre__ li__le

cro__ bo__le fri__ we__ sti__

pre__ing fi__ing fu__ pu__ ba__le

Now sort them into four lists.

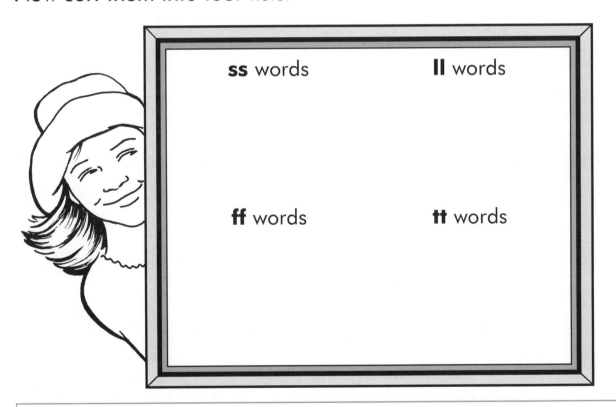

ss words

ll words

ff words

tt words

Finish these words so that they match the definitions.

All the answers have a double letter.

1 d _____ clothing worn by girls

2 l _____ another word for 'small'

3 s _____ the bones in your head

4 o _____ opposite of 'on'

name .... date ....

The **et** letter pattern frequently appears at the ends of words. Quite often it follows either **ack**, **ick**, **ock** or **uck**.

Make the words for each list, using a **ck** pattern + **et**
e.g. **r** + **ack** + **et** = **racket**

ack words	**ick** words	**ock** words	**uck** words
j _____	t _____	l _____	b _____
p _____	w _____	p _____	
r _____	cr _____	r _____	
	th _____	s _____	

What am I? My last two letters are **et**, but what is the rest of my word?

1 m _____   I attract other metals.

2 c _____   I'm a small cupboard.

3 t _____   I'm often taken to stop pain.

4 b _____   I'm a frilly hat.

5 c _____   I'm a summer game.

6 b _____   I carry water.

Write a sentence with each of these words.

upset _____

blanket _____

triplet _____

name _____ date _____

q is <u>never</u> written without u.

Examples: **qu**ick **qu**estion

Build these words. The first is done to help you.

qu + ick = _quick_   qu + estion + er = _____

qu + ack + ing = _____   qu + iet + ly = _____

qu + ick + ly = _____   qu + ilt + s = _____

squ + are = _____   squ + atter = _____

mo + squ + e = _____   mo + squ + ito = _____

Choose a word from the box to match each clue.

queen	quiz	square	squirrel	banquet
liquid	conquer	squeak	quart	quaint

1 two pints _____   6 a small animal _____

2 four-sided shape _____   7 fluid _____

3 to overcome _____   8 royal person _____

4 important meal _____   9 pretty _____

5 a noise _____   10 competition _____

Write a sentence with each of these words.

squabble _____

squalid _____

quality _____

name _____   date _____

The 'wo' sound is usually spelt **wa**. Examples: **wa**nt **wa**tch

Choose a word to match each clue.

wasp   washing   wand   watch   war
swamp   warren   swan   ward   wallet

1 a large water-bird   _____
2 a stinging insect   _____
3 a small timepiece   _____
4 boggy ground or marsh   _____
5 a slender stick   _____
6 a long fight   _____
7 dirty clothes   _____
8 part of a hospital   _____
9 container for money   _____
10 place where rabbits burrow _____

Write a sentence with each of these words.

warrior   _____

watchman   _____

swallow   _____

swap   _____

name _____ date _____

Some words with the 's' sound should be spelt with **c**. This is called a **soft c**. Check the spellings of these words using a dictionary. Tick the words that are correctly spelt, and correct the others.

sity	race	sentre	fansy	sinema
sycle	cansel	rice	bounce	entise
Desember	polise	danse	pounse	palase
	exsept	excellent	fase	

Choose a word from the box to match each clue.

> office cygnet pencil twice certificate
> century accident fence celery centipede

1 a place where secretaries work _____

2 an edible plant _____

3 one hundred years _____

4 two times _____

5 writing implement _____

6 creature with a hundred legs _____

7 railing to enclose land _____

8 unexpected happening _____

9 young swan _____

10 a signed document _____

name _____   date _____

Some words with the 'j' sound should be spelt with **g**. This is called
a **soft g**. Check the spellings of these words using a dictionary.
Tick the words that are correctly spelt, and correct the others.

jerm	anjel	page	energy
cabbaje	jiant	tragic	packaje
hinje	jiraffe	jentle	frinje
garaje	jinjer	vejetable	geography

Choose a word from the box to match each clue.

regiment gypsies strange agile urgent
gem large village cottage orange

1 a spherical fruit   _____
2 a small cluster of houses _____
3 a rare stone   _____
4 part of an army   _____
5 a small country dwelling   _____
6 unusual   _____
7 nimble and active   _____
8 needed in a hurry   _____
9 big   _____
10 travelling people   _____

name _____ date _____

d often comes before **ge** when it follows a short vowel.

Examples: c**a**ge (**a** = long vowel / no **d**)

c**ad**ge (**a** = short vowel / has **d**)

Copy the words in this box into the lists below.

cadge edge nudge porridge midget trudge
budget lodge badger wedge midge
ledge badge gadget hedge grudge
dodge judge lodger fudge bridge

Words with **short a**

_____
_____
_____
_____

Words with **short e**

_____
_____
_____

Words with **short i**

_____
_____
_____

Words with **short o**

_____
_____

Words with **short u**

_____   _____
_____   _____
_____   _____

name _____ date _____

i comes before e (when the sound is 'ee')

　　Examples: p**ie**ce, pr**ie**st

except after c

　　Examples: re**ce**ive, **cei**ling

or when the sound is not 'ee'.

　　Examples: r**ei**gn, h**ei**r, for**ei**gn

Copy the words in this box into the lists below.

achieve　leisure　shield　chief　deceit
their　brief　weight　believe　niece
grief　eight　neighbours　receipt

Words with the **ie** pattern

_____
_____
_____
_____
_____
_____
_____

Words with the **ei** pattern

_____
_____
_____
_____
_____
_____
_____

Now put a coloured dot next to the words with the 'ee' sound.

Write a sentence to say what you notice about the words with a coloured dot and the **ei** spelling pattern.

name _____   date _____

Sort the words in the box into three lists according to
their last two letters.

> postal table actual tunnel dental
> kestrel possible towel little

Words with **al** endings	Words with **el** endings	Words with **le** endings
_____	_____	_____
_____	_____	_____
_____	_____	_____

Now write two more words of your own to add to each list.

_____	_____	_____
_____	_____	_____

Choose a word from the box to match each clue.

> chisel mongrel hostel
> cathedral equal signal casual

1   tool for carving wood or stone   _____

2   large church building   _____

3   dog of mixed breeding   _____

4   place where people stay   _____

5   gives a warning   _____

6   relaxed   _____

7   same as   _____

name _____ date _____

The endings **en** and **on** sound the same.

Copy the words in the box into the two lists below.

> lesson ribbon kitten lemon happen seven
> pardon sudden reason button wooden
> oxygen golden prison skeleton cotton

Words with the **en** ending		Words with the **on** ending	
_____	_____	_____	_____
_____	_____	_____	_____
_____	_____	_____	_____
_____	_____	_____	_____
_____	_____	_____	_____

Now add two more words of your own to each list.

_____   _____

_____   _____

Choose a word from the box to match each clue.

> rotten   wooden   kitten   seven
> pardon   mutton   squadron   iron

1 sheep meat   _____   5 made of wood _____

2 a young cat   _____   6 a metal   _____

3 bad   _____   7 excuse   _____

4 a group of aircraft _____   8 six plus one   _____

name _____ date _____

Sort the words in the box into three lists according to their last two letters and write them below.

passenger burglar corridor visitor
motor doctor terror similar
customer calendar explorer
altogether laughter peculiar cellar

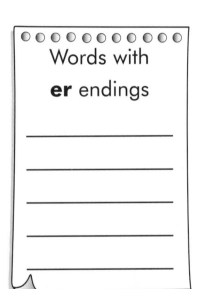

Words with **ar** endings

_____
_____
_____
_____
_____

Words with **er** endings

_____
_____
_____
_____
_____

Words with **or** endings

_____
_____
_____
_____
_____

Now add three more words of your own to each list.

_____ _____ _____

_____ _____ _____

_____ _____ _____

Write a word for each clue.

1 grows crops _____

2 educates children _____

3 works on ships _____

4 entertainer _____

5 writes books _____

6 mends pipes _____

name _____   date _____

Most words with the 'ee' sound at the end are spelt with **y** at the end. However, some end in **ey**.

Think of a word that ends with **ey** to answer each clue.

1 like a small horse   d _____

2 a game played with bent sticks and a ball   h _____

3 traditional meat eaten at Christmas   t _____

4 horse rider   j _____

5 animal that climbs trees and eats bananas   m _____

6 made by bees   h _____

7 takes smoke out of a house   ch _____

These words have their final **ey** or **y** missing. Use a dictionary to help you decide which list to write them in.

chutn_ sill_ countr_ voll_ batter_ bab_
journ_ chimn_ vall_ happ_ donk_ tumm_

Words with the **ey** ending	Words with the **y** ending
_____	_____
_____	_____
_____	_____
_____	_____
_____	_____

Silent letters

Learning targets

On completion of this section children will:

1 ➤➤ have become aware of 'silent' letters, and had the chance to learn the spelling of the more frequent words which contain such letters.

Before you start

There are various schools of thought as to what constitutes a silent letter. Some teachers, for example, might with some justification, class the modifying or magic 'e' as silent, or the 'gh' in 'igh'. However, for the sake of convenience, and in order to avoid as much confusion for the child as possible, the present course assumes that letters that contribute directly to forming a vowel phoneme are not strictly silent. So the 'silent' letters are those the omission of which would not directly impact on the pronunciation of that word in the context of the standard phoneme/grapheme relationships (see page 5),

e.g. 'write' ('rite' remains the same phonically, whereas 'writ' does not, the 'i' being a short vowel phoneme without the 'e' being present). However, 'g' as in 'resign' and 'b' as in 'tomb' are also treated as silent letters.

Background knowledge

Many silent letters are present in English as a result of the adoption and integration of words from other languages, (e.g. 'mortgage' = 'dead pledge' from Old French).

There are several letters that are found as silent letters more commonly than others. Each of these are dealt with in the units, but most work on silent letters will arise spontaneously as other literacy work is undertaken.

Teaching the units

Units 1–3   Copymasters 55–57

This section comprises 3 units:

Unit 1: **Initial 'k', final 'b'**   (Copymaster 55)

Unit 2: **Initial 'w', medial 'w'** (Copymaster 56)

Unit 3: **General review**   (Copymaster 57)

General teaching strategies

1   A popular way with the children to start a lesson on silent letters is to write on the board a short paragraph, such as:

I knew I'd enjoy our trip to the castle. To be honest I'm not sure which part was best. We listened to the guide who asked us whether

we had been before and whether we'd seen the king's tomb, or the beautifully carved white columns. The best bit was the climb to the top of the tower. After about two hours we left, but I know I'll go back again, hopefully in the autumn.

Invite volunteers to come forward and, in turns, to circle a silent letter.

Group or individual strategies

1   Use the copymasters as appropriate.

2   Ask groups or individuals to write their own sentences which contain words with silent letters.

Unit 1   **Initial 'k', final 'b'**

Useful family word groups

b (after m)

lamb, limb, bomb, comb, tomb, dumb, numb

climb, plumb, crumb, thumb

b (before t)

debt, doubt, subtle

initial **k**

knit, knob, knot

knelt, knack, knock

knee, kneel, knife, knew, know, known

knight, knuckle, knowledge

Unit 2   **Initial 'w', medial 'w'**

Useful family word groups

w (before r)

wrangle, wrap, wreck, wreckage, wretched, wriggle, wringer, wrinkle, wrist, write, wrote

w (before h)

whole, wholemeal, wholesome

w (after s)

sword, swordfish

answer

Unit 3   **General review**

Useful family word groups

h

wheel, whether, which, whisker, whisper, white

hour, honest, honour

rhyme, rhythm, rhubarb, rheumatism, rhinoceros

exhibit, exhibition, exhaust

g

reign, resign, design, sign

gnome

n

hymn, autumn, column, condemn

t

castle, listen, Christmas, thistle, whistle

Sort the words into two lists and write them below.

> lamb knit bomb knot comb
> knock dumb knee numb knew

Words with a silent **k**

_____
_____
_____
_____
_____

Words with a silent **b**

_____
_____
_____
_____
_____

Copy the words and draw a circle around the silent letter in each of them. The first one has been done for you.

know   knot   knight   knock   knelt

(k)now _____ _____ _____ _____

What do you notice about the letter after the **k**?

_____

Copy the words and draw a circle around the silent letter in each of them.

climb   bomb   limb   tomb   lamb

_____ _____ _____ _____ _____

What do you notice about the letter before the **b**?

_____

name _____ date _____

Copy the words and draw a circle around the silent letter in each of them. The first one has been done for you.

wrap   wriggled   written   wreck   wrist

(w)rap _____   _____   _____   _____

What do you notice about the letter after the **w**?

_____

_____

All the silent **w**'s have been left off the words in the list below.

Copy out the words, adding a **w** where it is needed.

Be careful, not all the words are misspelt!

rite   write

rinkly   _____

read   _____   reckage   _____

rist   _____   restler   _____

riggle   _____   rustler   _____

Write a sentence with each of these words.

sword   _____

wreck   _____

answer   _____

name _____   date _____

These words look wrong. All the silent letters have been left out.
Check the spelling of each of them. Copy out the words, adding the
missing letters. Use a dictionary to help you.

thisle	_thistle_	casle	_____
lisen	_____	colum	_____
clim	_____	thum	_____
onestly	_____	reumatism	_____
wispering	_____	holesome	_____
anserable	_____	reckage	_____
rubarb	_____	gost	_____
naw	_____	tonge	_____

Circle the silent letter in each word, then write a sentence with
the word.

wrench _____

resign _____

wrapped _____

whisker _____

whisper _____

rhinoceros _____

rhythm _____

Compound words, contractions and syllabification

Learning targets

On completion of this section children will:

1 ➤➤ understand the concept of compound words
2 ➤➤ have practised all the main contractions
3 ➤➤ have become aware of the concept of syllables.

Before you start

Words can be manipulated, built up and deconstructed in various ways. Various curriculum documents suggest children spend time looking for words within words. However, this should not be confused with compound words, contracted words or word syllables. 'Words within words', is not a linguistic concept, although it is a useful device for encouraging children to think carefully about letter combinations. Thus, 'start' can be said to encompass 'star', 'tar', 'tart' and 'art'.

Background knowledge

Compound words, in their simplest form, are nouns composed of two other nouns which together make a different word (e.g. 'lighthouse' is a combination of the two nouns 'light' and

'house'. Other kinds of words can also be combined to form compound nouns.

Contractions are also usually two (though sometimes one or three) words which are abbreviated in the spoken form. In writing this is represented by an apostrophe. The apostrophe marks the part of the word where letters have been omitted (e.g. 'I am' contracts to 'I'm'). On occasions there are variations on this (e.g. 'cannot' – one word – contracts to 'can't'; 'will not' contracts to 'won't' – notice the letter change).

Syllables are the 'units of pronunciation uttered without interruption forming the whole or part of a word'. Each syllable in a word contains a vowel phoneme and usually one or more consonant sounds (e.g. 'magic' has two syllables 'mag + ic').

Teaching the units

Units 1–8 Copymasters 58–65

This section comprises 8 units:

Unit 1: **Compound words 1** (Copymaster 58)
Unit 2: **Compound words 2** (Copymaster 59)
Unit 3: **Compound words 3** (Copymaster 60)
Unit 4: **Contractions 1** (Copymaster 61)
Unit 5: **Contractions 2** (Copymaster 62)
Unit 6: **Contractions 3** (Copymaster 63)
Unit 7: **Syllables 1** (Copymaster 64)
Unit 8: **Syllables 2** (Copymaster 65)

General teaching strategies

1 To introduce compound words, write the following clues on the board, omitting the words in bold:

finger + print = **fingerprint**

light *+ house =* lighthouse

pass + **word** *=* password

rail + way = **railway**

Ask the children to supply the missing single or compound words.

Invite volunteers to offer similar clues for other compound words.

2 Contractions might be introduced in a rather similar way. Write these examples on the board, omitting the letters in bold:

they **are**   they're

it **is**   it's

you **will**   you'll

Explain that the words in the second column are contractions. They are formed by combining the two words in the first column. Ask a child to describe what has been done to make the contraction. Emphasise that the apostrophe does not float about aimlessly, but is positioned exactly where the missing letter(s) would have been.

3 Point out that contractions are usually associated with informal language situations. They are not usually part of formal or official language. Write the following piece on the board, and ask for a volunteer to read it aloud, substituting contractions for the underlined words. Ask other children to rub out and replace the underlined words with contractions.

We are having a class Christmas party next Monday. We will invite the head teacher as she was not able to come last year. It will be fun. I am sure there will be lots to eat. Let us all think of games we would like to play.

4 Syllables can be understood only if the class has a firm grasp of vowel phonemes. Say your own name, or the name of a child, very slowly and clearly. Ask how many vowel sounds were heard. Follow by asking selected children to say their names slowly and deliberately to the class. Write each name on the board, and use them to distinguish between vowel letters and vowel sounds, e.g. Jane = one vowel sound, but two vowel letters. From this the concept of one vowel sound = one syllable can be developed.

5 Each child should have three pieces of paper, marked 1, 2, 3. Read the following words. After each word the

children should hold up the paper corresponding to the number of vowel sounds/syllables:

breeze bonnet children discover scratch teapot untidy unhelpful chair

6 Discuss the difference between syllables and finding words within words. Use the following words, and others the children might suggest, to undertake both tasks alongside each other to demonstrate the difference.

understand recording reinforcement basket architect chemistry

Group or individual strategies

1 Use the copymasters as appropriate.

2 Give the group a 'starter' word or words from which they have to create as many compound words as possible, e.g.

house: lighthouse greenhouse houseboat treehouse

3 A group or pair of children could make and play 'Contraction Concentration', a simple card game. On one card write a contraction and on another the words from which it was made (e.g. 'haven't', 'have not'). Make about 20 such pairs of cards.

a) Place the cards face down.
b) Each player in turn selects two cards, trying to make a matching pair.

If a pair is found the player keeps them and takes another turn.

c) Play until all the cards are matched and removed.
d) The winner is the player with the most pairs.

4 Write a list of words for the group, e.g.

hat own time thirty peppermint newspaper babies raining happiness happily knitting.

Divide a piece of paper into four columns. Write the words in the first column, the vowel letters they see in the second, the vowels they hear in the third, and the number of syllables in the fourth.

Units 1–3	**Compound words**

Reference chart of simple compound words and more advanced concepts of compounding words

1 Two words joined together

bedroom	fingerprint	homework	matchbox	spotlight
crossword	fireman	lampshade	playground	tablecloth
dartboard	flashlight	lighthouse	shoelace	
earthquake	foghorn	lipstick	showjumping	
farmhouse	football	manhole	skateboard	

2 Two words joined with a hyphen

by-product	high-class	know-all	man-made
dry-clean	high-flying	long-range	self-service
flat-footed	hitch-hike	low-lying	skin-tight
hard-hearted	hot-blooded	make-up	spin-off

3 Two separate words used together as a noun

crash barrier	ground floor	skimmed milk	tape recorder
cricket bat	ice cream	swimming bath	
Easter egg	living room	tape measure	

4 Words are sometimes combined with others to give a special meaning

Combining Word	Meaning	Examples
-proof	to give protection against	waterproof, fireproof, soundproof, bulletproof, foolproof
-free	without	carefree, dust free, germ free, trouble free, fat free (diet), salt free (diet), tax free
-mate	friend or fellow worker	playmate, schoolmate, workmate, shipmate, helpmate
-power	force	manpower, horsepower
-time		playtime, teatime, springtime, bedtime
-handed		right-handed, left-handed, single-handed, one-handed, double-handed heavy-handed
-shaped		heart-shaped, star-shaped, pear-shaped, kidney-shaped
-wise	in the manner of	crab-wise, crosswise, clockwise, lengthwise
-sized		man-sized, giant-sized, king-sized, good-sized, large-sized
self-		self-starting, self-propelled, self-taught, self-centred
cross-	across	crossroads, cross-stitch, crossbar, cross-current, cross-wind, cross purposes (opposed) cross examine
fore-	placed at the front	foreword (in a book), forehead, foremost, forefinger, forename, foreman
	before or earlier	forenoon, foresee, foretell, forecast

Units 4–6 Contractions

Reference chart of some more frequently used contractions

I'm, I'd, I've, I'll
you're, you'd, you've, you'll
he's, he'd, he'll
she's, she'd, she'll
it's, it'll
we're, we'd, we've, we'll
they're, they'd, they've, they'll
that's, there's, there'll
here's
who's, who'd, where's, what's, what'll
aren't, isn't, hasn't, hadn't, haven't
didn't, doesn't, don't, won't, shan't, can't, couldn't, wouldn't, shouldn't
how's, let's

Units 7–8 Syllables

No separate word lists are provided for these units. For practice see Copymasters 64 and 65.

name   date

The words in the box are compound words, made by joining two shorter words.

> play + ground = playground
> air + port = airport

Write the compound word made by joining these pairs of words.

birth + day = _____

fire + place = _____

down + stairs = _____

foot + ball = _____

shoe + lace = _____

snow + fall = _____

Underline the compound word in each sentence.
Then write the two words it is made from.

1 Is anyone in?   _____ _____

2 The boat went over the waterfall.   _____ _____

3 She loves to play netball.   _____ _____

4 Jan tripped over her shoelace.   _____ _____

5 I left it somewhere in the room.   _____ _____

Railway is a compound word, made by joining two shorter words, **rail** and **way**.

Write the two words that form these compound words.

weekend

_____ + _____

sunrise

_____ + _____

homemade

_____ + _____

skateboard

_____ + _____

notebook

_____ + _____

something

_____ + _____

Use two words from the box to form compound words to fill the gaps below.

> Sun   birth   foot   skate
> ball   day   board   day

1 _____ will be a special day.

2 It is my brother Edward's _____.

3 I have bought him a _____.

4 Mum and Dad have got him a _____.

Make two compound words from these short words and use them in your own sentence.

> after   snow   noon   ball

name _____   date _____

Make 10 compound words using the words in the box.

news under ring quick ear lace black
port paper pool ground loud shoe air
speaker every sand where whirl berry

_____   _____

_____   _____

_____   _____

_____   _____

_____   _____

Write a sentence to answer these questions.

A <u>ring</u> is 'a small, circular band'. What is an 'earring'?

_____

<u>Whirl</u> means 'to move in circles'. What is a 'whirlpool'?

_____

Since <u>port</u> means 'gateway', what is an 'airport'?

_____

A <u>paper</u> is a kind of document, so what is a 'newspaper'?

_____

A <u>berry</u> is a small fruit, so what is a 'blackberry'?

_____

Write four compound words that have 'where' as one of their
small words.

_____   _____   _____   _____

name _____ date _____

The words in the box are contractions, made by joining
two shorter words.

An apostrophe (') shows where a letter or letters are left out.

don't can't I'll isn't
she'll there's doesn't here's

Write the contraction made by joining these pairs of words.
The first one has been done for you.

do + not =
don't
_____

I + will =
_____

she + will =
_____

does + not =
_____

can + not =
_____

there + is =
_____

is + not =
_____

here + is =
_____

Underline the contraction in each sentence.
Then write the two words it is made from.

1 I'll see you at school.   _____ _____

2 I don't know the answer.   _____ _____

3 There's my house.   _____ _____

4 We won't see from here.   _____ _____

5 She'll be back soon.   _____ _____

name _____ date _____

Couldn't is a contraction, made by joining two shorter words, **could** and **not**.

Write the two words that have been joined to make these contractions. The first one has been done for you.

couldn't   wouldn't

<u>could</u> + <u>not</u>   _____ + _____

haven't   don't

_____ + _____   _____ + _____

you'll   you're

_____ + _____   _____ + _____

he's   we're

_____ + _____   _____ + _____

Rewrite each sentence, using a contraction instead of the words underlined.

<u>We will</u> need everyone here by two o'clock.

_____

<u>There will</u> be no excuses for being late.

_____

<u>I am</u> sure <u>we are</u> going to win today.

_____

<u>I have</u> heard <u>they are</u> not as good as us.

_____

Use the contraction **I'll** in your own sentence about what you hope to do this weekend.

_____

name _____   date _____

Write the contraction formed by each pair of words.

do not _____   they are _____

it is _____   she will _____

I am _____   I have _____

I will _____   could not _____

had not _____   there is _____

who is _____   were not _____

is not _____   does not _____

we are _____   will not _____

Write sentences using the contractions in the boxes.

Try to make your sentences make a continuous short story.

isn't _____

_____

won't _____

_____

couldn't _____

_____

I've _____

_____

we're _____

_____

there's _____

_____

name _____   date _____

A syllable is a part of a word that can be sounded by itself.

Every syllable has a vowel sound.

Say these words to yourself.

Write how many syllables you hear.

turkey (_tur_key_)   [2]   monkey   [ ]

garden   [ ]   fork   [ ]

finger   [ ]   kangaroo   [ ]

computer   [ ]   nose   [ ]

circus   [ ]   railway   [ ]

Write the syllables for each of these words.

happy	_hap-py_	silly	_____
birthday	_____	Thursday	_____
fourteen	_____	yesterday	_____
tomorrow	_____	Saturday	_____
unhappy	_____	impossible	_____

Choose four long words from a book, and write out the syllables in each.

_____   _____

_____   _____

A syllable is a part of a word that can be sounded by itself.

Every syllable has a vowel sound.

Say these words to yourself. Write how many syllables you hear.

apple (ap-ple) [2]   person [ ]

twenty [ ]   undone [ ]

frog [ ]   difficult [ ]

lorry [ ]   crocodile [ ]

Scotland [ ]   purple [ ]

Match a syllable in the first column to a syllable in the second column to make a word.

Ap	ing	_____	broth	cle	_____
hap	py	_____	gar	er	_____
morn	ger	_____	un	son	_____
fin	ril	_April_	per	den	_____

up	ly	_____	in	en	_____
sil	fore	_____	farm	cket	_____
be	rel	_____	giv	side	_____
squir	set	_____	cri	er	_____

Roots and suffixes, including plurals

Learning targets

On completion of this section children will:

1 ➡➡ have practised all the main spelling rules for creating the plural forms of nouns

2 ➡➡ have become familiar with the origins and usages of the main suffixes.

Before you start

The addition of suffixes to words is one of the most significant complications for children's early spelling. However, an understanding of the purpose of suffixes and the key spelling rules that relate to their application can alleviate many of the difficulties.

Background knowledge

Suffixes can be added to a word to change or modify its meaning (e.g. the 'er' in 'walker' changes the meaning, even though the root and the new word are related; 'walked' is a modification of the verb 'walk', signalling past tense).

Suffixes, as in the case above, can change the part of speech of a word, enabling roots to form and generate verbs, nouns, adjectives or adverbs (e.g. verb: 'enjoy'; noun: 'enjoyment'; adjective: 'enjoyable'; adverb: 'enjoyably').

It is also useful to consider at this point the implications of plural forms of nouns. Whilst the majority of plurals simply take an 's', there are other forms which can be confusing.

Suffixes also enable degrees of comparison, often helping to define comparative (comparison between two) and superlative (comparison between more than two), whether used as adjectives or adverbs.

For a summary of the key rules that relate to the application of suffixes and plurals see the main rules of English spelling on pages 7–8.

Teaching the units

Units 1–22 Copymasters 66–87

This section comprises 22 units:

General teaching strategies

1   It is not practicable here to give detailed plans for the introduction to each of the spelling patterns described in this section, though some broad guidelines might be helpful.

   a) Take small steps, grouping word families wherever possible.

   b) If there is a rule, use that as the focus of a lesson. Return to the rule as often as is necessary, particularly when it is possible to demonstrate using alternative examples.

   c) Reinforce using the LSCWC approach, even if a rule should be sufficient to guide the children.

   d) Be constantly alert, and encourage the children to be alert, to the parallels that can be drawn between making plurals or adding suffixes (e.g. what happens when a root word ends in 'y', whether making a plural or creating an adverb).

Group and individual strategies

1   When teaching plurals, give the children frequent opportunities to convert words, phrases and sentences from singular to plural. This affords help not only with the spelling, but also with the construction of the sentence, drawing attention to irregular plurals (e.g. 'foot'/'feet').

2   The best individual and group work will be developed from contexts driven by other more general literacy teaching. Use the copymasters to extend such opportunities, or for children who might need a more rigorous and structured approach.

3   A useful vehicle for drawing together and practising suffixes in a more isolated context, and a way that supports basic grammatical awareness, is the 'Word Tester'.

Offer the following chart, and encourage the children to find their own words to test and add to such a chart:

Verb	Adverb	Noun	Adjective
enjoy	enjoyably	enjoyment	enjoyable
play	playfully	playfulness	playful
irritate	irritably	irritation	irritable
agree	agreeably	agreement	agreeable

A helpful way for the children to check whether their suffixed word is correct is to put it into one of the following sentences:

Verb:	She may _____ this.
Adverb:	It was done _____ .
Noun:	I noticed her (its) _____ .
Adjective:	This is very _____ .

Units 1–8	**Adding 'ing' and 'ed'**

Refer to page 8 (Using suffixes) for details of the rules for changing tense by adding 'ed' and 'ing'.

Units 9–12	**Plurals**

Refer to page 8 (Making plurals) for details of the rules for pluralisation.

Unit 13	**Comparatives: 'er', 'est'**

simple addition of suffix

long, longer, longest
swift, swifter, swiftest
strong, stronger, strongest
sweet, sweeter, sweetest
weak, weaker, weakest
clean, cleaner, cleanest

doubling last letter

fat, fatter, fattest
sad, sadder, saddest
red, redder, reddest
hot, hotter, hottest
big, bigger, biggest

retain 'e' but don't double it when adding 'er', 'est'

safe, safer, safest
tame, tamer, tamest
brave, braver, bravest
fine, finer, finest
wise, wiser, wisest
loose, looser, loosest

Unit 14	Comparatives: 'ier', 'iest'

change final 'y' to 'i' before adding suffix

happy, happier, happiest
flashy, flashier, flashiest
pretty, prettier, prettiest
messy, messier, messiest
silly, sillier, silliest
risky, riskier, riskiest
frilly, frillier, frilliest
windy, windier, windiest
chilly, chillier, chilliest
bossy, bossier, bossiest
foggy, foggier, foggiest
rocky, rockier, rockiest
spotty, spottier, spottiest
frosty, frostier, frostiest
muddy, muddier, muddiest
funny, funnier, funniest
sunny, sunnier, sunniest
lucky, luckier, luckiest
dusty, dustier, dustiest

Unit 15–22	Common suffixes

Meanings, with examples, of the more common suffixes

Suffix	Meaning	Examples
able, ible	capable of being	eatable, edible, recognisable
an, ian	connected with	parliamentarian, publican, magician

ance, ence	state of	remembrance, resemblance, existence
ant	one who	assistant, servant, descendant
et, ette	little	casket, owlet, cigarette
et, eer, ier	one who	joiner, engineer, carrier
ess	female	mistress, princess, waitress
ful	full of	plentiful, meaningful, beautiful
fy	to make	beautify, purify, simplify
hood	state of being	childhood, knighthood, falsehood
less	without	careless, hopeless, meaningless
ling	little	codling, gosling, yearling
ment	state of	contentment, enjoyment, resentment
ock	little	hillock, tussock
ory	a place for	dormitory, factory, priory
ous	full of	courageous, famous, glorious

Unit 15	**Adverbs 'ly', 'ily'**

simple addition of suffix

swift, swiftly
serious, seriously
strong, strongly
sweet, sweetly
weak, weakly
clean, cleanly

retain 'e'

safe, safely
brave, bravely
wise, wisely
nice, nicely

change final 'y' to 'i' before adding suffix

happy, happily
angry, angrily
pretty, prettily

Unit 16	**Adding 'ful', 'less'**

simple addition of suffix

careful, dreadful, faithful, grateful, sorrowful, thoughtful, wonderful
careless, faithless, harmless, hopeless, thoughtless

change final 'y' to 'i' before adding suffix

plentiful, beautiful, dutiful, fanciful, merciful
merciless, penniless

Unit 17	Adding 'ness', 'hood', 'dom', 'ment'

simple addition of suffix

darkness, illness, weakness, likeness
improvement, agreement, judgement, punishment
kingdom, freedom, wisdom, random
boyhood, girlhood, parenthood, priesthood

change final 'y' to 'i' before adding suffix

laziness, ugliness, happiness, emptiness
likelihood

Unit 18	'sure', 'ture' endings

-sure
leisure, measure, treasure
closure, enclosure
pleasure, displeasure
composure, exposure

-ture
nature, future
lecture, picture, puncture
texture, fixture, mixture
sculpture, scripture
structure, fracture, manufacture
denture, venture, adventure
departure, signature
furniture, architecture

Unit 19	Greek suffixes

-phone (-phony)
telephone
saxophone
microphone
symphony

-graph (-graphy)
telegraph
autograph
photograph
paragraph
geography

-sphere
atmosphere
hemisphere

Unit 20	'able', 'ible' endings

-able

able, perishable, reasonable, dependable, agreeable, workable, laughable, miserable, loveable

-ible

horrible, terrible, possible, sensible, responsible, visible, forcible, incredible, edible, legible

adjectives dropping 'e'

value / valuable   cure / curable   desire / desirable
recognise / recognisable   believe / believable

Unit 21	'sion', 'tion' endings

-usion
transfusion, confusion
conclusion, exclusion, inclusion, seclusion, illusion, disillusion

-ision
vision, television, provision, supervision, revision
division, subdivision
decision, indecision, incision, precision
collision

-asion
invasion, evasion, occasion, persuasion

-osion
explosion, erosion, corrosion

-ersion
version, conversion, dispersion, diversion, immersion

-ension
pension, suspension, tension, extension, dimension, comprehension

-ansion
mansion, expansion

-ession
session
aggression, compression, depression, impression, progression
expression, oppression, suppression
obsession, possession
recession, concession, succession, procession
profession, confession

-ission
mission, admission, commission, omission, permission, submission, transmission

-ussion

concussion, discussion, percussion

-assion

passion, compassion

-ition

ambition, condition, edition, ignition, position, addition, partition, tuition
ammunition, competition, recognition, repetition, expedition

-ation

nation, station, ration
location, relation, vacation, celebration, conservation, conversation, education, explanation, occupation, operation, population, situation, vaccination, examination, investigation, multiplication

-otion

lotion, potion
motion, emotion, promotion, commotion
devotion

-etion

completion, deletion, discretion

-ption

eruption, disruption
deception, reception, interception
caption, option
description

-ction

action, fraction, traction
attraction, extraction, subtraction
section, connection, direction, election, infection, objection, selection
fiction, friction
distinction
suction, instruction
function, junction

-ntion

mention, attention, detention, intention, invention

Unit 22	**'l', 'll'**

care, careful, carefully	plenty, plentiful, plentifully
grace, graceful, gracefully	beauty, beautiful, beautifully
thought, thoughful, thoughtfully	duty, dutiful, dutifully
pain, painful, painfully	mercy, merciful, mercifully
help, helpful, helpfully	fancy, fanciful, fancifully
spite, spiteful, spitefully	

name _____   date _____

A suffix is added to the end of a word to change its meaning.

Add **ing** to each of these words to tell your reader that something is happening now.

Then write a sentence with each word.

jump   _jumping_

_____

dust   _____

_____

splash   _____

_____

fall   _____

_____

Before you add **ing** to each of these words you will need to double the last letter.

hop	_hopping_	mop	_____
swim	_____	trap	_____
run	_____	trot	_____
clap	_____	drip	_____
slip	_____	shop	_____

To add **ing** to a short word that does not end in **e**, first look at the letter before the last letter.

If it is a single vowel, double the last letter before adding **ing**.

If it is not a single vowel, just add **ing**.

Examples:

jog   jogging,   shop   shopping

Add **ing** to these words. Decide whether you need to double the last letter before adding **ing**.

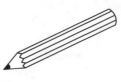

sit	_sitting_	slip	_____
slim	_____	hop	_____
hit	_____	fit	_____
sell	_____	chop	_____
cut	_____	shop	_____
tap	_____	let	_____
peck	_____	swim	_____
bat	_____	net	_____
drop	_____	nod	_____

name _____   date _____

To add **ing** to a short word that does not end in **e**,
first look at the letter before the last letter.

If it is a single vowel, double the last letter before adding **ing**.

If it is not a single vowel,
just add **ing**.

w, **x** and **y** are never doubled.

Examples:

j**o**g   jogging,

sl**ee**p   sleeping,

li**c**k   licking

Add **ing** to these words. Decide whether you need to double the last letter before adding **ing**.

dig	*digging*
spit	_____
beat	_____
tell	_____
hug	_____
suck	_____
tick	_____
bang	_____
wish	_____
press	_____

bath	*bathing*
walk	_____
fall	_____
jump	_____
shut	_____
shoot	_____
blink	_____
sing	_____
smash	_____
try	_____

name   date

> To add **ing** when a word ends with **e**, drop the **e** before adding **ing**.
>
> Examples:
>
> hop**e** hoping, div**e** diving

Add **ing** to these words. Decide whether you need to drop the **e** or whether or not to double the last letter before adding **ing**.

wave	*waving*	walk	*walking*
rake	_____	bounce	_____
kiss	_____	save	_____
stop	_____	skate	_____
graze	_____	blame	_____
dive	_____	hike	_____
slide	_____	pack	_____
win	_____	joke	_____
choke	_____	smash	_____
hide	_____	fly	_____
glue	_____	slip	_____

name .... date ....

A suffix is added to the end of a word to change its meaning.

Add **ed** to each of these words to tell your reader that something has already happened.

Then write a sentence with each word.

jump   <u>jumped</u>   _____

                  _____

dust   _____   _____

                  _____

splash   _____   _____

                  _____

walk   _____   _____

                  _____

Before you add **ed** to each of these words you will need to double the last letter.

hop   <u>hopped</u>   mop   _____

drop   _____   hop   trap   _____

drum   _____   hopped   trot   _____

clap   _____   ✓   drip   _____

slip   _____   shop   _____

name _____   date _____

To add **ed** to a short word that does not end in **e**, first look at the letter before the last letter.

If it is a single vowel, double the last letter before adding **ed**.

If it is not a single vowel, just add **ed**.

w, **x** and **y** are never doubled.

Examples: j**o**g   jogged, sh**o**p   shopped

Add **ed** to these words. Decide whether you need to double the last letter before adding **ed**.

pot   _potted_____

dip   _____

rip   _____

rub   _____

mug   _____

tap   _____

peck   _____

bat   _____

ban   _____

tax   _____

rob   _____

hop   _____

fit   _____

chop   _____

tow   _____

drill   _____

flap   _____

net   _____

nod   _____

slam   _____

name _____ *date* _____

To add **ed** to a short word that does not end in **e**, first look at the letter before the last letter.

If it is a single vowel, double the last letter before adding **ed**.

If it is not a single vowel, just add **ed**.

w, **x** and **y** are never doubled.

Examples:

j**o**g   jogged,

li**c**k   licked

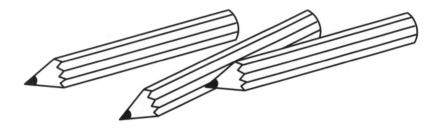

Add **ed** to these words. Decide whether you need to double the last letter before adding **ed**.

grab	*grabbed*	bath	*bathed*
slim	_____	walk	_____
kick	_____	slip	_____
spot	_____	jump	_____
drop	_____	shop	_____
suck	_____	stamp	_____
peck	_____	dress	_____
bang	_____	shift	_____
wish	_____	smash	_____
press	_____	trip	_____

name _____ date _____

To make the **ed** when a word ends with **e**, just add the **d**.

Examples: hop**e**   hope**d**

To add **ed** when a word ends with **y**, change the **y** to **i** before adding **ed**.

Examples: tr**y**   tried, fr**y**   fried

Add **ed** to these words. Remember the rules.

wave	*waved*	try	*tried*
rake	_____	bounce	_____
dry	_____	save	_____
stripe	_____	cry	_____
graze	_____	blame	_____
dive	_____	hike	_____
pounce	_____	spy	_____
fry	_____	joke	_____
choke	_____	race	_____
shove	_____	love	_____
glue	_____	hate	_____

name _____   date _____

Plural means 'more than one'.

To show the plural of most nouns, we add **s**.

Example: cat   cat**s**

To show the plural of nouns that end with **s**, **x**, **sh**, or **ch** we add **es**.

Examples: dre**ss** dress**es**,   bo**x**   box**es**

Write the plural forms of these nouns.
Remember the rules.

dog	_dogs_	bus	_buses_
rake	_____	bounce	_____
church	_____	fox	_____
elephant	_____	brush	_____
hill	_____	duck	_____
wish	_____	glass	_____
torch	_____	match	_____
bush	_____	six	_____
tree	_____	arch	_____
finger	_____	radish	_____
box	_____	lip	_____

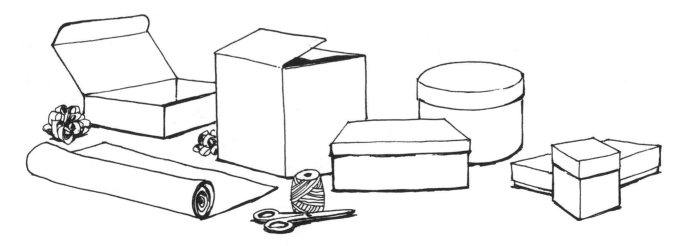

To make the plural form of a noun that ends with **y** change the **y** to **i** and add **es**.

Example: stor**y**   stor**ies**

But if the letter in front of the **y** is a vowel, simply add **s**.

Example: to**y**   toy**s**

Write the plural forms of these nouns. Remember the rules.

day	_days_	fairy	_fairies_
fly	_____	pony	_____
boy	_____	activity	_____
quay	_____	trolley	_____
valley	_____	alley	_____
motorway	_____	baby	_____
nappy	_____	berry	_____
jay	_____	lady	_____
penny	_____	cherry	_____
lorry	_____	way	_____
hobby	_____	posy	_____

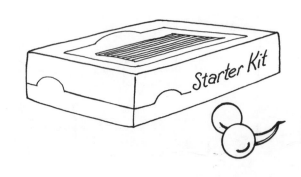

name .... *date* ....

To make plural forms of nouns we normally just add **s** or **es**.

Examples: broom broom**s**, brush brush**es**

To make the plural form of a noun that ends with **f** or **fe** we usually change the **f** or **fe** to **v** and add **es**.

Examples: wol**f** wol**ves**, wi**f**e wi**ves**

Write the plural forms of these nouns.

knife _____   thief _____

life _____   half _____

leaf _____   calf _____

loaf _____   wife _____

Write a short nonsense story about a family of wolves. Use as many plural words ending in **ves** as you can.

_____

_____

_____

_____

_____

name _____   date _____

To make the plural form of most nouns that end with **o** we usually add **es**.

Example: her**o**   hero**es** unless it ends with **oo**:
example: cuck**oo**   cuckoo**s**
or is a 'music' word, example: piano   piano**s**
or is a shortened form, example: photo**s**, rhino**s**, hippo**s**

Write the plural forms of these nouns.

hero   _____   motto   _____

cockatoo   _____   hippo   _____

radio   _____   bamboo   _____

shampoo   _____   echo   _____

soprano   _____   photo   _____

cello   _____   rhino   _____

potato   _____   tomato   _____

Write a plural version of this silly sentence.

The hero sat on a bamboo stall eating a tomato whilst taking a photo of a hippo and a rhino fighting over a potato.

The heroes _____

_____

name _____ date _____

When we want to compare two things we usually add **er** to an adjective.

Examples: long   long**er**,   old   old**er**

If there are more than two things to compare we usually add **est**.

Examples: long   long**est**,   old   old**est**

Finish these groups of adjectives.

	+**er**	+**est**
short	_____	_____
high	_____	_____
slow	_____	_____
tall	_____	_____
deep	_____	_____

To add **er** or **est** to a short word, if the letter before the last letter is a single vowel double the last letter before adding **er** or **est**.
w, **x** and **y** are never doubled.

Examples: fat   fat**ter**   fat**test**

Finish these groups of adjectives.

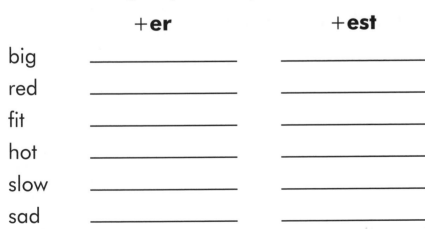

	+**er**	+**est**
big	_____	_____
red	_____	_____
fit	_____	_____
hot	_____	_____
slow	_____	_____
sad	_____	_____

name _____ date _____

When we want to compare two things we usually add **er** or **est** to an adjective.

Examples: long   long**er**   long**est**

But if the adjective ends in **y** we change the **y** to **i** and add **er** or **est**.

Examples: happy   happ**ier**   happ**iest**

Finish these groups of adjectives.

	+**er**	+**est**
merry	_____	_____
funny	_____	_____
jolly	_____	_____
silly	_____	_____
lazy	_____	_____
sleepy	_____	_____

Write a sentence using each of these adjectives.

busiest _____

nastiest _____

hungrier _____

lazier _____

name _____   *date* _____

When we want to describe actions, we often add **ly** to a word to make an adverb.

Example: quick   quick**ly**

But if the word ends in **y** we change the **y** to **i** and then add **ly**.

Example: happy   happ**ily**

Make an adverb from each of these words.

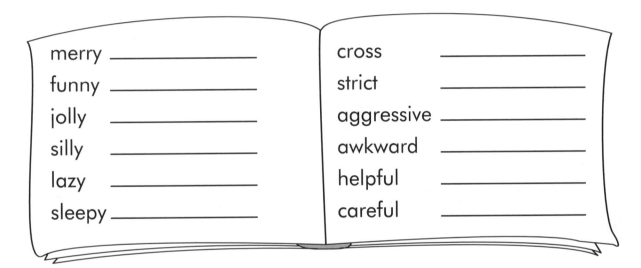

merry _____   cross   _____

funny _____   strict   _____

jolly _____   aggressive _____

silly _____   awkward   _____

lazy   _____   helpful   _____

sleepy _____   careful   _____

Make an adverb from each of these words and use it in a sentence.

busy   _____

_____

nasty   _____

_____

hungry   _____

_____

lazy   _____

_____

kind   _____

_____

name   date

A suffix is used to change the meaning of a word.

The suffix **-ful** means 'full of', 'able to' or 'the amount that will fill'.

Examples: hope**ful**,   help**ful**,   spoon**ful**

The suffix **-less** means 'without' or 'not able to do'.

Examples: hope**less**,   harm**less**

Choose a word from the box to match each definition.

colourless beautiful joyful flavourless
meaningful careless effortless endless

not taking care _____   needing no effort _____

without any colour _____   full of joy _____

full of beauty _____   without ending _____

lacking flavour _____   full of meaning _____

Write the antonym (opposite) of each of these words.

careless   _careful_   meaningful _____

joyless   _____   hopeful   _____

doubtful   _____   harmless   _____

helpful   _____   powerless   _____

82

name	date

A suffix is used to change the meaning of a word.

Suffixes such as -**ness**, -**hood**, -**dom** and -**ment** change verbs and adjectives into nouns and some nouns into different nouns.

Examples: happi**ness**, man**hood**, king**dom**, improve**ment**

Remember to change **y** to **i** before adding a suffix.

Change these words to nouns by adding -**ness**, -**hood**, -**dom** or -**ment**.

ill	_____	content	_____
free	_____	neighbour	_____
like	_____	advertise	_____
pay	_____	child	_____
encourage	_____	dark	_____
courageous	_____	helpless	_____
mother	_____	disappoint	_____
treat	_____	judge	_____

Make a noun from each of these words and use it in a sentence.

entertain _____

_____

ugly _____

_____

treat _____

_____

like _____

_____

name _____ date _____

ure is an important spelling pattern. Usually, **ure** follows either **t** or **s**.

Sort the words in the box into two groups and write them below.

measure   departure   picture   architecture
sculpture   pleasure   exposure   moisture
nature   pressure   leisure   treasure

sure words   **ture** words

_____ _____   _____ _____

_____ _____   _____ _____

_____ _____   _____ _____

Add two more of your own words to each group.

_____ _____   _____ _____

The words above have either **ure** as a suffix
or it is part of the root word.

Make lists of the two sorts.

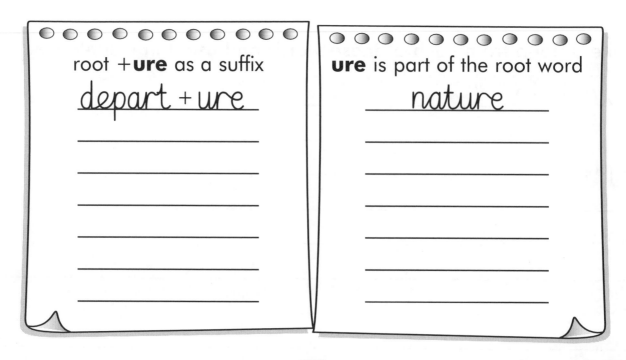

root +**ure** as a suffix

depart +ure

_____

_____

_____

_____

_____

ure is part of the root word

nature

_____

_____

_____

_____

_____

name _____ date _____

Suffixes that have a **ph** were originally Greek words.

phone Greek for 'voice' or 'sound'
graph Greek for 'writing'
sphere Greek for 'ball'

Choose a **ph** suffix to complete each of these word beginnings, and write what the complete word means.

auto _____
_____

hemi _____
_____

micro _____
_____

atmo _____
_____

photo _____
_____

tele _____
_____

para _____
_____

name _____ date _____

Adding **ible** or **able** to a verb can make it into an **adjective**. **able** is much more common than **ible**, so you are safer using it if you are not sure!

ible is usual when the antonym (opposite) begins with an **i**.

Examples: respons**ible**   irrespons**ible**, mend**able**   unmend**able**

When adding **ible** or **able** to a word ending with **e**, we usually drop the **e** first, unless the ending is **ce** or **ge**.

Examples: lov**e**   lov**able**,   noti**ce**   noti**ceable**

Add either **ible** or **able** to these word beginnings.

	beginning + **ible** or **able**	antonym
vis	_visible_	_invisible_
work	_____	_____
cred	_____	_____
reason	_____	_____
desire	_____	_____
notice	_____	_____
believe	_____	_____

Complete this table. Write the correct suffixes for each word.

root word	+ **able** or **ible**	+ **ably** or **ibly**
argue		
cure		
suit		
horror		
disagree		
manage		
rely		

name _____ date _____

Abstract nouns (things we can't see, touch, hear, taste or smell) often end with **tion** (e.g. 'position').

They are often made by adding **tion** to a verb (e.g. **relate** (verb) **relation** (noun)).

Use a dictionary to help you make an abstract noun from these verbs.

relate	_relation_	observe	_____
create	_____	evaporate	_____
calculate	_____	prepare	_____
situate	_____	operate	_____

Write the verb that is related to each of these nouns.

Be careful, some of the words are quite different.

relation	_relate_	solution	_____
opposition	_____	pollution	_____
calculation	_____	reception	_____
direction	_____	detention	_____

Many nouns end in **sion** rather than **tion**.

Make nouns from these verbs.

express	_expression_	discuss	_____
revise	_____	provide	_____
expand	_____	include	_____
confuse	_____	extend	_____

name   date

ll is a common letter pattern.

Examples: all, bill, fill, full, usefully

but the suffixes ful or fil have a single l.

Examples: fulfil, useful

The suffix **ful** added to a noun can make an adjective, and the suffix **fully** can make an adverb.

Make the adjectives and adverbs from the nouns below.

Remember, if you are adding **ful** or **fully** to a word ending in **y**, first change the **y** to an **i**. (duty dutiful)

noun	adjective	adverb
care	*careful*	*carefully*
grace		
thought		
pain		
deceit		
help		
spite		
sorrow		
wonder		
dread		
beauty		
plenty		
mercy		

Roots and prefixes, including antonyms

Learning targets

On completion of this section children will:

1 ➤➤have learnt the main spelling rules governing the addition of prefixes to root words

2 ➤➤be more familiar with the origins of the main prefixes.

Before you start

The addition of suffixes to words (see Section 7) can be a complication for children when spelling, but the use of prefixes is not difficult to master.

Background knowledge

For a summary of the key rules that relate to the application of prefixes see page 8 (Using prefixes). But the key is simple – if in doubt, just add it!

The main function of prefixes is to indicate the opposite meaning, or antonym.

Many prefixes have early and/or foreign derivations, and their meanings are described in the table on page 154.

Teaching the units

Units 1–6 Copymasters 88–93

This section comprises 6 units:

Unit 1: **Prefixes 'un', 're'**   (Copymaster 88)

Unit 2: **Prefixes 'un', 'dis', 'in', 'mis'**   (Copymaster 89)

Unit 3: **Prefix 'al'**   (Copymaster 90)

Unit 4: **The prefix rule**   (Copymaster 91)

Unit 5: **Greek prefixes 1**   (Copymaster 92)

Unit 6: **Greek prefixes 2**   (Copymaster 93)

General teaching strategies

1 The table on page 154 indicates a cross-section of the most frequently occurring prefixes. There are others, but the principle for, and manner of, their usage remains the same.

In the early stages it may be simplest to consider the very common prefixes simply as familiar letter clusters, but soon the fact that each carries a meaning will prove a powerful teaching focus.

2 The role of the prefixes in creating the antonym of a root word is a helpful place to put the early emphasis. Write on the board a list of words that can take a negative prefix, and ask children to suggest the correct prefix.

3 Write a list of words which carry a prefix. Ask volunteers to define each word by defining first the root or base word, and then the prefix.

Group and individual teaching strategies

1 Use the copymasters as appropriate.

2 Many dictionaries give a definition for the main prefixes, and details of their origins. Set groups or individuals the task of researching a selection of prefixes and listing a number of words which carry each prefix. The children could then define the prefixes or use them in sentences that indicate their meaning.

| **Units 1–6** | | **Common prefixes** |

Prefix	Meaning	Examples
a	on/in	aboard, afloat, ashore
a, ab, abs	away, from	avert, abdicate, absent
ad, ac, at, etc.	to	admit, accept, accede, attract
ante	before	antecedent, anteroom
anti	opposite, against	antibiotic, antidote
aqua	water	aquarium, aquatic, aqualung
auto	self	autobiography, autograph, automobile
bi, bis	two, twice	bicycle, bigamy, biscuit
circum	round	circumference, circumvent
con, com	together	connect, compete, convene
contra	against	contradict, contrary
de	a) down, away from	descend, depress, decline
	b) reversal	deactivate, defrost
dia	through, apart, across	diagonal, diagram, dialogue
dis	away, not	discharge, disappear, disagree
ex	a) out of	extract, export, excursion
	b) formerly, before	ex-Prime Minister
fore	previous, in advance	forecast, foretell, foresee
im, in	a) in, into	import, incision, include
	b) not	immovable, impractical, incapable, incorrect
inter	between	international, interval, intervene
micro	small	microbe, microscope, microphone
mis	wrong, wrongly	misconduct, mischief, misbehave
mono	alone, single	monorail, monocle, monopolise
ob	a) open, clear	obvious, observe
	b) against	obstruct, object, obstacle
post	after	postpone, postscript, p.m. (post meridian – afternoon)
pre	before	precaution, prepare, preface
pro	a) in front of, forward	proceed, progress, propeller
	b) in favour of	profess, prophet, propose
re	a) again	reappear, retake, repeat
	b) back	return, retrace, rebate
sub	under	submarine, subway, subsonic
super	over, beyond	superior, superhuman
tele	far	telescope, television, telephone
trans	across	transfer, transport, transatlantic
tri	three	tricycle, triangle, triplets
un	not	unimportant, unsafe, untrue
vice	acting for	vice-captain, vice-admiral, viceroy

Some support word lists and notes for reference when teaching 'negative' prefixes

un

unhealthy, unsuccessful, untrue, unbelievable, unwilling, unemployed, unwanted, unknown, uncertain, unconscious, unfortunate, undo

en

encourage, enclosure, enlist, enthusiastic, entangle, enable, enlarge

in

inconvenient, incomplete, independent, inequality, infrequent, invalid, insufficient, insensitive, incorrect

im

impossible, improbable, imperfect, impassable, impertinent, impatient

dis

disable, disadvantage, disagree, disappear, disapprove, discharge, discolour, disconnect, discourage, dishonest, dislike, dislodge, disloyal, disobey, displease, disprove, disqualify, disregard, distrust

de

defrost, defuse, deface, decompose, detour, deform, degrade, defraud

Note: 'un' is the most common prefix of those that indicate a negative. It is used to indicate the opposite and occurs with verbs ('untie', 'unlock'), with adjectives ('unjust', 'unfriendly') and with adverbs ('unwisely'). 'un' derives from Old English; its Latin equivalents include 'en' and 'in', which when used with a word beginning with 'm', 'p' or 'b' becomes 'em' or 'im'. (e.g. 'impossible').

negative 'sense'

discriminate, disaster, disease, dismal, distress, disturb, dismal, disgust

decay, deceive, defend, defy, destroy, desperate, despair, desolate

name _____   date _____

A prefix is added to the beginning of a word to change its meaning.

Add the prefix **un** to each of these words.

Then write the meaning of the new word.

safe	*unsafe*	*not safe*
happy	_____	_____
even	_____	_____
fair	_____	_____
tie	_____	_____

Add the prefix **re** to each of these words.

Then write the meaning of the new word.

lay	*relay*	*to lay again*
open	_____	_____
use	_____	_____
heat	_____	_____
test	_____	_____

Write a sentence that has the word 'unusual'.

_____

_____

_____

name _____   date _____

Add the prefix **un** or **dis** to each of the words in brackets to make a word to fill each gap.

The magician made the white rabbit _____ . (appear)

The little animal seemed _____ of what was happening. (aware)

We tried to _____ where it had gone. (cover)

When it came back it was _____ . (harmed)

My mum said she _____ animals being made to perform. (liked)

I said I _____ as long as they weren't upset or hurt. (agreed)

Add the prefix **in** or **mis** to each of these words.

Then write the meaning of the new word.

visible	_____	_____
understand	_____	_____
correct	_____	_____
complete	_____	_____

Write a sentence that has the word 'misplaced'.

_____

_____

name _____ date _____

'All' means 'everyone' or 'everything'.

But the prefix **al** is spelt with only one **l**.

Write the meaning of each of these words.

Use a dictionary if you need to.

almost _____

_____

almighty _____

_____

always _____

_____

already _____

_____

Choose four words from the box and write a sentence for each one.

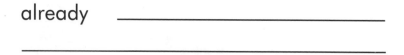

although almost already
also altogether almighty always

1 _____

2 _____

3 _____

4 _____

All right is always two words!

name .... date ....

When you add a prefix to a word, just do it!

Don't worry if this doubles some of the letters.

Add the prefix **un** to each of these words.

_____necessary   _____natural   _____tidy

_____intentional   _____named   _____nerve

Add the prefix **over** to each of these words.

_____run   _____reach   _____ripe

_____react   _____look   _____rule

Add the prefix **dis** to each of these words.

_____service   _____satisfy   _____trust

_____obey   _____similar   _____appear

Add the prefix **im** to each of these words.

_____mobile   _____modest   _____mature

_____movable   _____measurable   _____possible

Now underline those words where the last letter of the prefix is the same as the first letter of the root word.

Write a sentence that has, if possible, one word from each of these prefix groups.

_____

_____

_____

name _____ date _____

Many prefixes came to English from the Greek language.

The prefixes below all came from Greek.

Look in a dictionary and find six words that begin with each one.

auto _____ _____ _____

_____ _____ _____

tele _____ _____ _____

_____ _____ _____

dia _____ _____ _____

_____ _____ _____

mono _____ _____ _____

_____ _____ _____

Look at the meanings of some of these words in a dictionary and then write what you think each prefix means.

auto _____

tele _____

dia _____

mono _____

name _____ date _____

Collect three words beginning with each of these prefixes.
Write the words in each group in alphabetical order.

auto

_____
_____
_____

trans

_____
_____
_____

sub

_____
_____
_____

bi

_____
_____
_____

aqua

_____
_____
_____

tri

_____
_____
_____

circum

_____
_____
_____

micro

_____
_____
_____

ex

_____
_____
_____